VOLUME ONE

Spiritual Journeys

Arlin E. Nusbaum

Spiritual Journeys

Volume One

Arlin E. Nusbaum

ISBN 1-60135-570-X

© Alpha & Omega Publishing

Spiritual Journeys 1

Table of Contents

Addendum

Introduction

He was born (1963) and raised in the Mormon faith, yet not in heavily Mormon-populated areas: Casper, Bakersfield, Houston, and Denver. He served a mission in Australia (the Melbourne Mission) and attended Oklahoma University (Norman OK) before and after his mission.

He has nine siblings. His mother converted to Mormonism before marrying his father, who was raised Mormon. All on his side of the family were Mormon, going right back to New York City when their first ancestor (David White Rogers) was converted by Elders Parley P. Pratt and Elijah Fordham.

Shortly after he returned from his mission, he married his first wife (from Australia) in the Salt Lake Temple. They had three children and lived in Australia for several years before their divorce. He returned to the United States, and when he was 29 years of age, he married his second wife (her first marriage) in the

Oakland CA, Temple. They lived in the Bay Area until he resigned from Mormonism the following year (he was Elders Quorum President at that time).

He and his wife, Tammy, have four children and have lived primarily in Modesto CA, after a short stint in Salt Lake City. None of their four children were raised in the Mormon Church.

Journey 1 - Being Raised Mormon

Being raised Mormon could absolutely be considered a spiritual journey, for Mormonism is all about God, the next life, etc. It is a highly structured religion, and there are rites of passage that young men and women go through, which may or may not be interpreted by them as "spiritual." Youth Camp is a rite of passage where the older kids take the opportunity to warn the younger ones about the perils of straying from God.

One such testimony greatly impacted Arlin because an older youth shared how he had strayed from God and experienced many bitter things, but after turning back to God, God forgave him, and his peace was restored. His testimony was sincere, and the Spirit of God touched everyone present. A second encounter happened when Arlin, as a newly ordained priest, blessed the sacrament. While for many priests this was a duty or something during which they may even laugh, Arlin says that the Spirit of God came upon him and assured him it was no light matter.

Because of that experience, he has always had the greatest respect for the sacrament.

No doubt other Mormons have had similar experiences, but what is important is to remember and honor each one.

Journey 2 - Mission

Journey 2 is about mission life, both the preparation, and the serving. Arlin always wanted to serve a mission, even though his father and an older brother and many Latter-Day Saint friends did not. He's not sure why, but it was never a question in his mind that he would serve. Perhaps it was the keen awareness of his standing with God (i.e., his conscience) that prevented him from backing away from doing what all young Mormon men were expected to do, even commanded to at that time.

How a young man approaches his mission can be like how they approach the sacrament—as a duty. They would complete the task, but they might not take it seriously or mock it while doing so. Or, like Arlin experienced with the sacrament, they might treat it with reverence and a fear of God. Perhaps the greatest influence regarding his mission preparation were other missionaries he split-off with during his preparation in Denver where he lived, and Oklahoma

9

while at college. Some young men were slackers, and he saw that, but others were in it with all of their hearts; they were clearly engaged in a spiritual battle for the souls of men.

It was particularly these elders in Norman OK who befriended him, shared with him, and encouraged him to prepare in a mighty way. Arlin had no transportation at college, so the missionaries would take him to church and other activities. He, in turn, would go with them to their appointments and, together, they brought several people into the church including a Jehovah's Witness, the son of Baptist minister, a Jew, and others.

For Arlin, this was a glorious yet challenging juncture. While he was spending so much time in spiritual encounters, it was bringing to him a bright recollection of his sins. Whether it was God pulling on his heartstrings or his own conscience, he was faced with his offenses, which caused him to sincerely fast and pray seeking God's forgiveness.

One time while on his knees in deep prayer and meditation in his dorm, an angel appeared to him in glory.

According to Arlin, this angel was so bright, and his glory radiated so deeply into him that it further contrasted and highlighted just how dirty his soul was from his past offenses. It was too much for him to take and Arlin begged that the angel leave. He believes it was meant to be a visitation for comfort but instead was interpreted by him as exposure and sorrow. Many days and several weeks passed in this state of gloom and despair, so he determined to go to his spiritual leader, the Bishop, and confess every sin he could recall. Remember, his determination was to get right with God before going on his mission.

There, in that bishop's office, he began to pour out his soul and confess all his sin with great sobs and remorse. It was at that moment that Jesus appeared and, with his finger to lips, said: "I have been watching you and am aware of all your prayers." Arlin looked at the Bishop, and then back at Jesus and wondered how it was that he could clearly see Jesus and hear Him, but the Bishop could not (or if he did notice, he did not say anything). Jesus went on to say that He could not console him at that time but would continue to watch and monitor his repentance process.

The Bishop did not excommunicate or disfellowship him, but he did forbid him from taking the sacrament or praying in meetings and other priesthood duties. He was then sent to the Stake President, who happened to be the director of the Institute where he had been taking classes. Between the two of them, they put Arlin through an arduous repentance process. It was a hard and embarrassing time, but they each assured him that when it was all said and done, his sins would be gone and peace restored.

The school year finished, and Arlin went on his mission. It was there, above a fruit shop, in a dirty old apartment with broken windows and no bed, that he received the results of what he calls a "trial of his faith." Successfully making it out on his mission and not falling into sin or just quitting out of fear or selfishness was all part of his test. Successfully out on his mission, overlooking thoughts of going home early, at last, the promised forgiveness and peace came. As he prayed, the Spirit of God came mightily upon him, lighting upon every cell in his body and piercing every inch of his soul.

This was the "Baptism of Fire" spoken of in Scripture, and Arlin experienced it firsthand. This lasted for 3 days as all filth was purged from his vessel—body, mind, and spirit. With this baptism came gifts of the Spirit. Not only could he see into the spirit world, he could see demons, departed loved ones, and angels. However, he says the Mormon theological view of such things was woefully inadequate to explain what he saw; the spirit world is far more complex.

The Gift of Prophecy was also activated in him, and he prophesied many things, including the death of Elder Bruce R. McConkie, the new church Hymnal, financial changes, a new temple in Melbourne, and consolidation of church meetings. His mission was, thus, more challenging and exciting than most. He brought in triple the number of converts than the mission average and says he requested an extension to stay longer on his mission (at that time they were only 18 months), but it was refused.

Here are some of his mission experiences. A missionary will sow seeds, harvest the seeds others have sown, or do both—sow and harvest. Each is equally important, the sowing and the harvesting. For example, he and his companion were riding the train one day and the Spirit said to him "Go talk to that girl." So, doing what missionaries learn to do all the time, he approached her and talked with her until he and his companion left the train at the next stop. He sowed the seed, and another elder baptized her and later thanked Arlin for paving the way. He never saw that girl again.

The precise opposite happened at a later time. He transferred to a new area and there was a single mother and her daughter whom many missionaries had taught, befriended, and done everything they could think of to get her into the waters of baptism—no one had succeeded. When Arlin met them, the Spirit immediately told him that they needed to follow through and be baptized or a worse fate would befall them.

The elder in leadership (District Leader) over Arlin and his companion had the same witness and he arranged for a surprise baptismal service (knowing she would not be baptized otherwise; she was too shy). Only her closest member friends were invited and the elders in leadership over the District Leader (i.e., Zone Leaders) were also present. Shortly into the meeting, this sister was informed that they were really gathered for her surprise baptism (she was greatly liked and the entire Relief Society room was filled), but she would not budge.

There were doubters in the meeting, including the zone leaders. Once they saw she was not going to be baptized they became very upset and threatened Arlin, and left. Slowly one-by-one nearly all lost faith and left, when in came an unknown woman into the room, who quietly sat down next to this sister and began to speak to her in her native tongue (East Indian). After speaking with her, she willingly consented to be baptized, both her and her daughter. Arlin says it was a joy-filled and Spirit-filled baptism that ended with great elation. The zone leaders returned and apologized for threatening Arlin, as well as the members the following Sunday.

It was discovered later that the mystery woman was prompted by the Spirit to stop everything she was doing and immediately go to that chapel. She said the prompting and leading were so strong, she quickly obeyed. She knew right where to go, what room to enter, and who to talk to. Arlin says miracles like that only come after a trial of one's faith. This dear sister avoided a pending "worse fate" and never regretted entering the waters of baptism.

Another experience similar to that one happened in the same area. Following the promptings of the Spirit where to tract, Arlin was led to a particular house. Inside were two divorcees who had three children (ages 9-12) between them. This was a chance to unite them into a family. The mother was highly motivated to do what was right and the boyfriend was tolerating their teachings. As per usual, they asked many hard questions of Arlin and his companion and each one was matched with strong and profound answers e.g., Is God real? Is there life after death? etc.

Their next appointment was three days away but then the Spirit warned Arlin to get to their house immediately and not wait. Arlin was told the devil had just given the father a deceptive dream that was meant to deter him from learning more about God or anything else. Arlin's companion warned him not to go or the father would become very angry with them and they would lose them as investigators. Arlin assured him if they did not go immediately they would be lost anyway, so they went.

Sure enough, the father was quite angry and was verbally abusive, but Arlin stood his ground and confronted him in front of the mother and told him about his dream and what it truly meant. They became astonished like King Nebuchadnezzar was when the prophet Daniel revealed to him his dream. Arlin demanded they let he and his companion in to bless the home and put this evil down. The father apologized and with the pleading of the mother, let them in. After peace was restored he and his companion left.

To bring this couple and their children into the waters of baptism they would need to get married. This was no easy task and the devil fought them every step of the way. One morning on their way to church, they never made it past their front porch. According to the mother, they were ready to go to church and when she stepped out the front door she was shoved by unseen hands off the porch and broke her leg; they never made it to church that day.

After church Arlin and his companion went to see why they did not attend and they were informed of everything. There the mother sat with a cast on her leg, shocked, and alarmed, and the husband was very silent. He had learned that the adversary was dangerous; they were in a fight not just for their lives, but their souls and their children. The Spirit prompted Arlin to fight back by blessing her and God would heal her leg. Arlin's companion anointed her and Arlin did the blessing.

This dear sister reported afterward that as Arlin blessed her she felt angelic hands come upon her leg and the healing power of God flow into her, and she knew her leg was healed. They eventually did overcome all hurdles, were married in the Mission Home, and they and their children all entered the waters of baptism. An elder who witnessed these events said to Arlin "You came to Australia for this family."

God did have a plan, and early in his mission Arlin says the Lord spoke to him and said: "You have two paths before you, one is toward leadership where you will end up as Assistant to the President, and on the other path you will find all the people you are to help." Arlin says he chose the latter path and was motivated to find everyone he was to teach. For example, before his mission, he had a vivid dream of a house on a particular street. He knew it was important, but not why, until one day after he had been out for more than a year he tracted down the very street he had seen in his dream.

There he was, standing at the top of that street and before starting down he said to his companion, "I don't know what's going to happen, but we are going to find someone very important on this street." Sure enough, a fourth of the way back up the street, they met a man who was highly ranked in the military who had become estranged from his family. He was a broken man who was willing to do anything to get back in the good graces of his wife and children.

Arlin marveled that God knew about

this man a year (or more) before and had shown Arlin in a dream. The full memory of that dream came flooding in. Within three days Arlin and his companion taught and baptized this brother before he attended a single church meeting. This was about repentance, forgiveness, and a new start and because of Arlin's prior witness, he assured others it was the right thing for this man.

There were other times when he saw a whole group of missionaries being too aggressive to get baptismal numbers up and he refused to take part. Sure enough, the prematurely baptized immediately fell away from the Church. Wicked missionaries who didn't care for the souls of others were a reality Arlin had to deal with on his mission. He witnessed missionaries who ran over mailboxes, took long sightseeing trips, shopped all day, grew beards, recorded music, lived with girlfriends, went swimming, went to the gym daily, did drugs, got involved in gang warfare, engaged in homosexual acts, etc.

With one of his companions, the Lord told Arlin to warn him that after he left to split-off with another companionship, if he was lazy while he was gone, God would judge him and he would become deathly ill. Within a few days after being away, Arlin received a phone call from the Mission Home informing him that his companion had taken deathly ill and had to be flown to the hospital and he would be assigned a new companion.

When he was with hardworking companions he says they could do much good. With one such companion they prayed for guidance and were led to a new town where, as far as they knew, missionaries had never been. With ease, they were led by the Spirit to a particular street and a particular house and there inside was a stay-at-home mother whom God wanted to bless in a great way. She was eventually delivered from drug addiction, spiritual oppression, and her marriage and family were saved after entering the waters of baptism. God loves the tender hearts of His daughters and the family unit.

Just walking down a street Arlin said he could see demons flee. Once, he and his companion were led to a street and particular house right at the precise moment that a Satanist was assisting the woman inside to curse her ex-husband. Arlin saw a powerful demon in her house, who brought it there, and what it was being commissioned to do. Arlin was shown all of this in Spirit from a distance, and when he and his companion knocked on the door the two ladies just inside the door stood in disbelief. After their arrival the house shook, the demon fled, and the owner of the house was put on notice not to give in to the promises of the Satanist.

On five different occasions, Arlin says the Lord used spiritually mature and gifted people to prophesy to him about his future. Only one was a church member, the others were not. These prophecies are too sacred to share, but again, it was God's plan for him to teach or be taught, to help or be helped. This two-way exchange happened often. One Sunday morning the Spirit instructed him to fast that day, with no explanation why.

So, Arlin fasted and waited upon the leading of the Spirit. That evening he and his companion were called to go to an inactive member's home to bless an expectant mother.

She was having difficulties in the later stages of her pregnancy and there was cause for alarm. Arlin then knew why he was instructed to fast. The mother was sincere and was praying for help. Arlin says the Spirit came upon him in a strong way and revealed many things to the mother including the fact that she had been secretly smoking cigarettes, and then the sex of her baby was revealed. She was greatly surprised that he knew she had been smoking. He was instructed to warn her, that if she did not live right before God from that moment on she would lose her baby.

Both she and her husband humbled themselves before the Lord and asked Arlin and his companion for a blessing. With arrogance, his companion wanted to do the blessing but Arlin reproved him saying, "God called me to a fast and has prepared me to bless her." Arlin laid his hands upon her (she was bed-ridden) and God's Spirit entered the room and flowed into her giving her great comfort, and everyone present received a witness of the love of God. In return, she showed Arlin something she considered sacred: a Polaroid picture of her baptism. In it could clearly be seen a shaft of light coming down upon her.

Even while he was on his mission the Lord was giving him information to bless others when he returned home. At his homecoming speech he said: "I have a message for someone in the audience, the Lord wants me to tell you ____." After the meeting a father came forward and said to Arlin, "That message was for me. I have been struggling with ____." Life is about service and being in the loving service of our fellowman. A mission was the prefect time to learn this lesson.

Journey 3 - Married Life

When two souls merge, there will always be joy and sadness. Joy to have someone with you and sadness that you don't have as much "me time." Depending on how committed each party is to the marriage will determine how fast (if ever) they adapt to life with their spouse. Married life should be their top priority, with extended family, friends, and careers second. If the marriage comes second, third, or fourth, the other spouse will suffer.

To whom will the suffering spouse turn during said times of betrayal and neglect? If that spouse is being true to their marriage, they will turn to God, which is a right everyone has, married or not. In his first marriage, Arlin had to turn to God a lot for support and guidance. And when children came, the need to turn to God increased exponentially. Seeking the will and help of God in such an unfortunate marriage could greatly endear one to God. Having been separated from his Australian family on more than one occasion, God gifted him the means to both see and visit his family in spirit.

Journey 4 - Children

Once the children are raised and gone it is easy to forget those early longings for a child, the prayers for and anticipation of them. It consumes a couple day and night, for weeks, months, and possibly years. If they are prayerful, God may grant them answers or insights. This could range from futuristic visions of a child to come, a dream, or even a visitation by the spirit of a child yet to be born.

In Arlin's case, he was blessed to not only have one of his children appear to him, but to accompany him for three months before the child was born. This, he says, was a soul that had just been created by God and immediately sent. It did not have a language or vocabulary. The teaching of this soul in its early stages began in pictures being telepathically exchanged, which slowly moved into sounds and words. How this helped or benefited this child is not clear to Arlin yet, but the Mormon idea that we live as spirit beings before we are born and have a pre-existence wherein we demonstrate a stewardship was debunked. That's not to say some spirits have not spent time in Heaven before coming to Earth, but what percent that may be is not known. God is still creating souls all the time.

Journey 5 - Spiritual Window

After some time had passed after his first marriage ended, Arlin began dating again and found himself in a precarious situation. There he was with a girl, alone, and all of a sudden a dimensional window opened and he saw a table with four men seated behind it. The two on the right were for his righteousness, and the two on the left for his demise. Nothing was said; they just watched. Arlin misinterpreted this as a sign to "go ahead." That was incorrect; it was a warning. Sometime later, he found himself in a similar state with a different girl. That same dimensional window opened, with the same number of judges behind a table. This time, he did not fail, and he has not seen that window and its judges since. From this experience, he said, he learned just how closely we are being watched.

Journey 6 - Repentance

Of course the transgressions committed with the misinterpreted vision had to be fully repented. His first time of full repentance occurred at college before his mission and covered many things from his childhood through his teens. This second need to repent was centered around that transgression, but because he was so devastated that he'd gotten off track, he did a thorough purge of all sins, whether great or small. This, he says, was achieved with the help of the Holy Spirit, which is able to bring "all things to our remembrance."

Again he fasted and prayed much and confessed the sins to his bishop. Ten years had passed since he had been to a bishop because of sins. This bishop, likewise, did not excommunicate or disfellowship him, but forbade him from partaking the sacrament or praying in church. Again, both restrictions caused him great embarrassment. Something that did not occur during his first formal repentance was the being "turned over to the buffetings of Satan." This was God's own punishment and had nothing to do with the bishop.

This, he says, was the worst time of his life. In that punishment, God's Spirit, the Holy Spirit, plus all angels of God are removed, and Satan's angels have full control. The great suffering came from not feeling part of anything, as God's presence was removed. He says it is like feeling lost in space, floating endlessly without having any sense of origin or direction (spiritually and mentally speaking).

Most humans never question their existence. They know they are on Earth, there are humans, the sun will rise, there is life and death, etc. But without God's Spirit to reference all those parts of one's existence, there is nothing but mental and emotional darkness, a void; a person truly feels "lost" and "abandoned." Coupled with constant demonic attacks, he was not able to sleep or eat and went to the bishop several times to ask for a priesthood blessing to stop the attacks.

Though he tried, no prayers or priesthood prayers helped. God had determined a time of punishment, and nothing but God would be able to restore His presence and bring the abandonment and attacks to an end.

Two long weeks went by before the end came, but the full repentance process took longer. In said cases, there are two types of forgiveness: one from the church, which church leaders control, and the other from God, which God alone controls. Sometimes the two parallel each other, but not necessarily. For Arlin, he would hike high into the hills above Palm Springs after work each day repenting, crying, and pleading with God. The hot summer heat was the exact punishment he felt he deserved. Each day he would hike higher, and on the day that he would receive the forgiveness of God, he climbed to the highest point of all.

Mt. Forgiveness, 33°44'52.3"N
116°27'15.2"W

He sat on the edge of a cliff at the highest point overlooking the desert floor (at no time did he ever bring water; it was a time of suffering and punishment). He took off his boots and poured out his soul for forgiveness, one last time. Then God descended in a cloud of glory over him and filled every inch of his soul with His Holy Spirit and power, bathing his soul, soothing, filling, and purifying. After a period of time, he was healed and filled.

Then God opened to his view a screen and showed him his future, or the future He was planning to give Arlin. The Scriptures say God will or can make "all things new" (Rev.21:5). Arlin learned firsthand this applies not just to the heavens and the Earth, but also to each of us.

God told Arlin that he would sell his home within two weeks, job transfer to San Francisco, find a new wife, and other related details. All that God showed Arlin came to pass. Then years later, when he and his wife were living in Salt Lake City, he witnessed this same miracle in the life of another person. One day they happened to be at East Canyon State Park when a modern-day pioneer handcart party arrived to rest before traveling into the valley.

It was quite a scene watching these long-distance travelers come to that spot before entering the valley. There were individuals and families; each walked passed them on their way to use the public restrooms at the park. There were wagons and horses and a temporary camp being fashioned just across from the park. One particular gentleman, who wore a hat and sunglasses, walked right past Arlin, used the restroom, then emerged and sat on the grass. As he walked, Arlin said he noticed a set of angels accompanying the man. After he seated himself in the shade, the Lord said, "Watch what I am going to do for this man."

What then unfolded was not unlike what he himself had experienced just a few years before. This man had strayed from God at great cost and went on this Pioneer Trek to suffer and repent, much like Arlin had journeyed into the desert mountains in the summer heat without water. God had been dealing with this man the whole way, taking him through his sins and chastising him along the way. Now, at the near completion of the journey, God wiped this man's slate clean and showed him in vision, just like he had Arlin, a new life. God can truly "make all things new." He is God.

Journey 7 - Antelope Island

Something else that happened during his brief stay in Utah occurred at Antelope Island. He and his family wanted to be able to say before returning to California that they had "floated" in the Great Salt Lake. While out there he noticed that the area was nearly void of the energy pollutions of man and evil spirits. For someone who sees into the spirit world, he says this was a rare occurrence. The Lord said to him, "I want you to camp here tonight and show you something." So Arlin returned home and made preparations to camp on the island that night.

The camping spots were entirely barren: no trees, no grass, nothing but bugs.

Nevertheless, he readied himself for what the Lord wanted to show him. Right at that time there came overhead a chariot, or what would be called in modern language *a starship*. Inside where two men from the Morning Star ("watchers" if you will) who were stationed in the nearby mountains and on a routine mission.

As they hovered overhead, the one said to the other, "He sees us; no one has seen us before. Let's go down and talk to him." The other person who seemed to have more seniority, said, "It is not allowed." And then they left. The junior partner was taken by Arlin's willingness to communicate, and so he continued to correspond with Arlin in spirit for the rest of the week, as time would permit. He showed Arlin their home in the mountains, their living quarters, etc. Arlin was surprised to see that they need R&R just like us and have a pool and other such amenities like us. The Lord showed Arlin how He had permitted them to rendezvous with certain individuals there at Antelope Island. One was a political figure, and the other was a scientist. In both cases, they were taken aboard their starship, flown around the city and taught and shown what the Lord wanted them to know. The Lord said to Arlin, "There should be a marker placed in remembrance of these events," because they are what would lead to a revolution in the sciences having to do with energy.

Journey 8 - Inspiration Point

Journey 8 is similar to *Journey 7*. Arlin and his young family lived for a time on a ranch in the hills above Orinda CA. During their first tour through the hills above Berkeley, Arlin saw where messengers of God had met with a professor from UC Berkeley. When Arlin asked his friend the name of that prominent hill, he was told it is called *Inspiration Point*. The official story behind that point is not known to Arlin, but he was shown that a piece of metal was given to this professor and it was meant to take science and humanity into the next level of their evolution. Arlin was told this was the impetus behind the creation of Lawrence Livermore Labs.

Many decades have passed since these helps were given, and whether they have been used to aid humanity, as intended, is not known. There are other spiritual journeys that Arlin does not want to share at this time, but suffice to say, God does use technology, and our governments know this and have been using it. Our

Journey 8 - Inspiration Point

Earth is full of the remnants of highly advanced societies, and he says it's time to give it another try.

Journey 9 - Saltair

During his short time in Utah, Arlin had other spiritual experiences and/or observations. The Lord said to him once, "I want you to visit Saltair. I have something to show you." Saltair was a place of extravagant parties and dances that peaked in the Mormon community of Utah at the start of the Industrial Age. So Arlin drove west of Salt Lake to where Saltair remains, and the Lord took him back in time and showed him what a big affair it was.

Latter-Day Saints would come by train all dressed up, and it was a great time of partying. He showed Arlin that just as technology advanced, so did industry and investments. This, He said, was when Mormons and the rest of the world went after *mammon* and *materialism*; he literally was shown the trains, the people, their dancing, etc.

Journey 10 - Kimball

Arlin did not always live close to a Mormon Temple (except for a brief time in Oakland), and so while he was in Salt Lake City, he took the opportunity to go to the temple multiple times each day. He noticed, and was surprised, by the number of times there was a complete void of Spirit and angels within the temple. There were times when there was dark energy and religious spirits running rampant. The drudgery by which many temple workers worked allowed for demons of all types (sexual and otherwise) to prey upon their minds, this alone prevented it from being a truly holy experience, aside from the positive emotions and energy generated by attendees with *their* expectations of holiness.

The temple rituals with the least positive spirit were confirmations, giving the priesthood, and the sealing of dead relatives. On one occasion, Jesus affirmed to Arlin that He had visited Lorenzo Snow in the lower hallway, an upper hallway, a meeting room where the leading brethren would meet, and He often accompanied President Kimball. No one walked so humbly with the Lord as did President Kimball, so it was no wonder that the ban on blacks receiving the priesthood was halted during his tenure as president.

Journey 11 - Serpents

But all was not rosy in Utah. There is a mystery lurking in the mountains of Utah which most, but perhaps not all, people would find bizarre. The Bible is clear that a "serpent" tempted Eve and was forced to go "on its belly" from that time forward. Such creatures still exist, and enough people have seen them to keep their legend alive. Most people will never come face-to-face with them, and so this Journey is of little value to the masses, but for the sake of those living in the mountains and near fresh-water lakes, he wants them to know they are not alone in what they know.

www.anw.com/kesara

This drawing by Kesara as described by Pamela Stonebrooke is, according to Arlin, an accurate depiction.

Journey 12 - Records Department

On one occasion Arlin observed a starship hover over an unknown building in downtown Salt Lake City, and several brothers from the Morning Star entered into the building and took copies of the software or records. He was curious to see what this building was and it had no markings on it whatsoever.

Journey 13 - Max Skousen

While Arlin was living in Salt Lake, the late Max Skousen (the lesser known brother of Cleon Skousen) was making radio and physical appearances, challenging whether the Saints truly loved God. Arlin observed that Max Skousen appeared as a bright light compared to the general darkness that pervaded the Salt Lake valley. Only by this contrast could one see how dark the rest of the populace was. This is a general observation and should not be interpreted as a condemnation of all members or people in Salt Lake, even though the membership IS under a churchwide "curse" (DC 84:50).

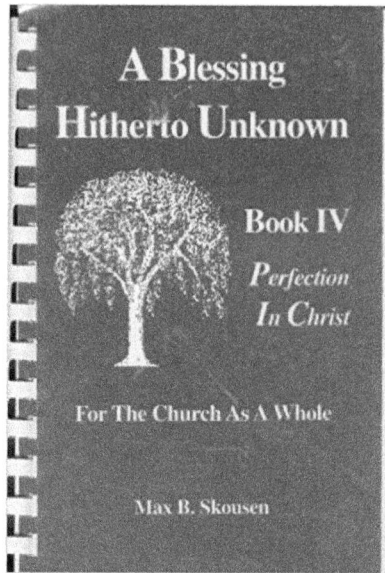

Journey 14 - Polygamy

As Arlin traveled home to California from Salt Lake, he began to read from a book he found called *Gospel Problems* (1920) by Heber Bennion. He says the author claimed to be sincere in his accusations against the church, but when it got to the part on polygamy, the author appeared to Arlin and said that polygamy was of God and that he must at once begin to abide by it. Shortly after this, even though the subject had not been discussed with Arlin's wife, she said she could accept the concept because it was commanded in the Doctrine & Covenants. A friend of hers said she would be willing to do it as well, for the same reason.

The author's visit, plus these "signs" where supposed to sway Arlin into embracing polygamy. The problem, according to Arlin, is that polygamy appeals to the lust of the flesh and is contrary to the Book of Mormon. Also, the deceased author did not come in the glory of God but was acting as a rogue agent. From this and other experiences,

Arlin learned that polygamy is a tool of the devil, and anyone who claims it is of God, and should be practiced or teaches that it is a requirement to live with God is woefully deceived and should repent and listen to the true Spirit and messengers of God.

It is no accident that nearly all defectors of the Mormon Church soon take up polygamy. Arlin believes it's a sure test that someone is being led by mischievous spirits. It is not part of Salvation or Exaltation and never was.

Journey 15 - Books

Arlin visited one of the oldest bookstores on the West Coast that was permanently closing its doors, in the hopes of finding a very old Bible, which he did. While he was browsing through other shelves, he came upon a set of green canvas–colored books, and the minute he picked them up, he suddenly saw a group of spirits come into the room. When they saw that he could see them, they quietly said something among themselves and left.

The books were part of the "I AM" movement, and the spirits were deceivers who know the location of each book and when one is handled. Their task is to infiltrate the minds of readers and imitate the voice of God as they read. From this and similar experiences with channeled books from the dead and extraterrestrials, Arlin says entire spiritual movements have been launched by deceiving spirits and beings who monitor their books and follow the readers, whispering in their ears and leading them down long-

involved   deceptive   paths   and
movements.

Journey 16 - New Age Church

Similar to Journey 15, Arlin says that during his mission he tracked into a church that claimed to perform healings and other miraculous things. He says it used to be a nice protestant church but had been taken over by a New Age group. When he and his companion entered the church, they noticed that the light through the beautiful stained glass windows had been blocked, and it was dark.

The pastor, a woman, claimed to know who they were but for some reason was not able to perform her usual psychic feats. That night Arlin says two spirits visited him and said they were sent from the pastor; she was extending a formal invitation to join her church as her assistant pastor. He refused their offer and sent them on their way in the name of the Lord Jesus Christ. Since that time he has discerned a great many counterfeit works; most are very elaborate and well supported in spirit. Some of the brightest minds in this life were just too smart for faith in God, and many of them are in league with movements on the other side that are meant to "show God up" by leading people astray.

Journey 17 - Jesse Duplantis

©JDM

In 2015 I went to a leadership training seminar at *Jesse Duplantis Ministries* in Destrehan, Louisiana. I had been a follower of Duplantis' writings and teachings for years. I first learned of Jesse when Our Lord directed me to a used bookstore and to a copy of his book entitled *Close Encounters of the God Kind*. That's how I came to learn about Jesse, and I had no idea that he was a famous Christian TV Evangelist. In his book Jesse shared many amazing experiences including: a visit from Jesus (in power), a tour of Heaven, his car being supernaturally transported, healings, etc.

As I am writing this, it just occurred to me that those experiences and any he shares on his program or when he travels are from *decades* ago, and he has no recent evidence that God is currently working through him in similar ways today (keep this in mind as you read the rest of this *Journey*). I say this because if a person were to look at the life of Joseph Smith, he too had remarkable experiences, but those were all early on and I am not aware of any evidence that God used him to perform any miracles, whether a healing or anything else the later years of his life.

I attended this seminar with the hopes of connecting with people and learning how best to market my Christian books. To help prepare for this event I conducted a seven-day fast. What I am going to share next is an appraisal and condemnation of not just Jesse's ministry, but *many* Christian ministries. The meetings all have the same format with an exciting worship group, loud music, and singing. There is nothing wrong with that in my opinion, but it can override the simple whispers of the Spirit and mask the spiritual with emotions, and I dare say, it is a crutch used by many to disguise or hide that which they lack—the Spirit of God.

Whether being in the ministry for decades is an acceptable excuse for growing stale and using things to disguise what you lack is questionable. I don't think it is fair to introduce the public and new Christians to emotions instead of the true Spirit of God (for this they will have much to answer for). After the people are stirred emotionally (and no doubt some, because of their own righteousness and humility are truly spiritually moved), then out comes the minister, guest speaker, etc. At this event, Jesse and his wife Cathy emerged and continued with the existing fervor by encouraging attendees to "pray in tongues" which created a great deal of what I would call "noise."

It is almost comical to witness in spirit

the spiritual "noise" or bedlam that was being generated, but because of my love for Our Lord, His servants, and fellow Believers I felt a great deal of concern and pity instead; it was very disconcerting to say the least. Through the sea of pandemonium of 500 (mostly) willing participants walked Jesse and Cathy, laying hands, giving words of knowledge and the like. It seemed to me they were looking for those most ready, who could easily be triggered to fall out (i.e., become slain in the Spirit) or breakout in "unknown tongues," both of which can be legitimate responses to a sudden influx of the Spirit.

But when they came to someone who needed that which cannot (usually) be generated from within—a true healing— they avoided the person entirely. In other words, I witnessed an elderly couple who came with the hope of having the husband's eyesight restored. Twice they approached Jesse and each time he avoided them and even had an assistant pastor lay hands instead. My heart ached for this couple who truly believed in the claims of Duplantis (whether by book or tape) of walking in God's power. They appeared to be sincere not desperate. In any case, this scene repeated itself for 9 sessions over 3 days.

Personally, I could not take it anymore and had to finally leave before returning for the final session. Between the uproar of tongue-speaking and when Jesse or a fellow minister would speak, they would take-up a collection and from these 500 souls in attendance Jesse exclaimed that he "believed" we would donate a whopping 5 million dollars! To me this was outlandish and further proof how disconnected he had become with the real world. Yes there may have been multi-millionaires in the audience who could have donated 1 or more millions of dollars, but even for them, this is an unusually high amount. Only on rare occasions do we ever hear of a single million dollar donation to any ministry (and they are usually good at making it known too).

I found it odd that Jesse had so much

security; I mean, he is only a minister of Jesus Christ right? They all looked like ex-military and highly capable of putting down the worst of threats. I counted at least 10 men who were both in disguise in the audience and in the aisles, and no doubt there were plenty more. I thought to myself, between the camera crews and security staff alone for those 3 days and 9 sessions he was going to need a significant amount of money just to cover their expenses. I could have given a pass to all that, but in all his preaching, the thing he preached on the most was money, and he bragged and bragged as if to assure attendees that he is worthy of it all and can be trusted with it, etc.

The preponderance of messages centered on money and wealth, and I know he has been preaching the same message for decades. I can appreciate this in a balanced fashion, but like Joseph Smith (and many successful ministers) he has gone beyond his original call and is building a kingdom on earth of great wealth and not assisting the poor or those in need:

4 For there are certain men crept in unawares, who were before of old ordained to this condemnation, ungodly men, **turning the grace of our God into lasciviousness,** and denying the only Lord God, and Our Lord Jesus Christ. (Jude 1)

In addition to my physical observations, I would like to share what I spiritually saw beyond the spiritual commotion that I already described. Keep in mind that I had been fasting for 7 days which for me is a lot because I live an already fasted life as a Vegetarian (30+ years). I had arrived early and fasted and prayed in my Motel room for several days before the event even started. The spiritual oppression I was met with was tremendous and I was greeted with loud booming thunder and lightning strikes and constant rain for several days. Initially I did not know what to make of it: was it focused on me, was it just the area, etc. I was so engaged with my own assignment that I did not pay too much attention to it because I have to deal with evil spirits all the time;

they are that prevalent today.

The physical obstructions I was faced with during this trip were many but I shall not further burden the reader with such mundane things. I'm sure most readers have experienced similar obstructions when trying to do the right thing. Because evil is present everywhere, Satan can, does, and will use any of a number of people to harass and thwart the plans of Believers; we have targets on our backs. That's not to say we are to be a sticking cushion for every demon that comes along, we are allowed and authorized to engage the enemy, take authority over them, and put them down (easier said than done, but it can be done).

When I entered the sanctuary at Jesse Duplantis Ministries I did not at first see the angels of God, but instead a very powerful spirit hovering over the sanctuary, positioned in the rear and high-up. This greatly troubled me for all throughout the event I saw that he was in control. No matter what was going on, he was present and strong. Now most churches have angels over them that can be seen stationed over them, some prophets claim there is an angel over "every church" but that has not been my experience (and I'm not sure why I haven't seen an angel over every church).

After 2 days of spiritual chaos I could not endure it further so left to take a break until the final session. I drove down by Jesse's house because it had received quite a bit of media attention, it being so large and funded by the public because it is listed as a"clergy house" and therefore free of any property tax. I drove past his house and along the Mississippi River passing one historic plantation after another when Our Lord interrupted my leisurely drive and instructed me to turn into the next plantation.

There, for the first time during this trip, under some large majestic oaks did I finally receive some spiritual reprieve from the constant barrage of oppressive forces. Because I was still fasting, I was very weak and highly sensitive to the slightest change in energy or spirit. The Lord then instructed me to take a tour of the plantation. The tour brought me to a highly protected document room that had special lighting to protect the several authentic documents inside.

One document that was signed by President Thomas Jefferson and Secretary James Madison was not lit until the tour guide flipped a switch. The next display was likewise not lit until my guide flipped a switch and then a most dramatic display took place, for the minute the light came on an original oil painting of the owner of the plantation was revealed and simultaneously the spirit of that man came very forcefully upon me. The Lord then spoke and said: "This is the portrait of the man whose spirit you saw in Jesse's church."

This startled me to say the least, for what I thought was going to be a physical reprieve from the heat and humidity turned out to be for something far more important! This man was *Jean Noel Destréhan (1754–1823)* owner of the **Destrehan Plantation** I was touring:

> After the Louisiana Purchase, he served as Speaker of the territorial House of Representatives from 1804 to 1806 before receiving an appointment from President Thomas Jefferson to serve on the Orleans Territorial Council. Destréhan served in this position during 1806 as president of the council. President James Madison

appointed him to a second legislative council for Orleans Territory in 1811, where he served again as president...He served in the Louisiana State Senate from 1812 to 1817 (*Wikipedia*).

I shall not go into the history of this man only to say that he was a wealthy land and slave owner who wanted more and more power and thus after he passed, he continued in that vein and still holds many as "slaves" and followers in the spirit world as we speak. Yes, spirits can wander, harass, or do their own thing in the world of spirits after they pass—that is until the Day of the Lord when the wicked will be judged and removed, both among the living and in the world of spirits. Those who sold their souls and served Satan in life go to their master, or hell and suffer there. Those who loved God, go to God. We go where our heart is until that glorious *Day of the Lord*.

The dead are looking for recruits among the living all the time and their greatest hope is to fool a living person into believing they are hearing God's voice, when in reality it is the voice of the deceased. When this happens they can be hooked into listening to that person instead of God for the rest of their life. Jesse is not entirely hooked by this man except when it comes to growing his ministry. Whenever he pondered what to do there in Destrehan, this powerful man who knew Destrehan like the back of his hand and who had a spirit of growth and power easily infiltrated the heart and mind of Jesse Duplantis. To show this is so, consider the look of Jesse's new house and see how similar it is to Destrehan's:

There were no redeeming qualities of Jesse and his ministry that I could spiritually see at that time. One of the things the adversary likes to do is demonstrate their control over a soul by having them do unusual and down right embarrassing things. In Jesse's case, it IS unusual for a minister to spend such large sums on a house for just him and his wife (34,986 square feet largest in the parish of Destrehan. Michelle Stuckey, "Watchdog group investigates Jesse Duplantis' lifestyle," *St. Charles Herald Guide,* June 04, 2010, http://www.heraldguide.com/details.php?id=7355). Had that elaborate house been built for the citizens, the seniors, the youth, the homeless, etc., it may have been justified.

To show how Jesse embarrassed himself

(his wife, his staff, and ministry) I share the following example:

> Jesse was bragging that his ministry has experienced no sexual improprieties whatsoever and to prove it, he went into great detail about being in a sauna alone when a naked woman walked in and laid down next to him. His wife Cathy begged him not to share the story and he replied to her "shut up woman" and kept talking. Everyone in the audience felt very uncomfortable with how he spoke to his wife and what he shared, after which he exclaimed, "I've seen hundreds of women naked." Wow, very sad that he would brag about something like that, including that he had an **11 year old girl friend when he was 19** (of course he was not a Believer at that time and thus could not be chastised for that, or could he?).

He did offer the following prophecy

which did not come to pass:

> This year, 2015, His glory will be
> revealed, in the flesh, and everyone
> will know God in their flesh...It will
> be like on Mt. Sinai.

I wish it were an accurate prophecy, it
sure was exciting at the time, which may
be why he said it, I don't know. Truly
God will reveal His glory and whether He
keeps pushing the timing back and this
was a true prophecy we may never know.
For the rest of this journey up until
somewhere over the Continental Divide
(while in the plane) the spirit of Mr.
Destrehan finally stopped harassing me.
It may be hard for people to grasp how
departed spirits can be allowed to go
rogue and continue to garner followers
and power in the next life, but there is no
difference between them and Satan and
his followers who are doing the same
right now.

I believe the reason why the spirit and
influence of Destrehan could go no
further is because he is somehow tied to

his time as overseer of the *Louisiana Territory* which bordered the Rocky Mountains:

©*Macmillan/McGraw-Hill*

Scriptural support for this dynamic can be found in Daniel when an angel was sent to answer his prayer but it could not reach Daniel because an entity called "the prince of Persia" held him up:

> 12 Then said he unto me, Fear not, Daniel: for from the first day that thou didst set thine heart to understand, and to chasten thyself before thy God, thy words were heard, and I am come for thy words.
> 13 **But the prince of the kingdom**

> **of Persia withstood me one and twenty days:** but, lo, Michael, one of the chief princes, came to help me; and I remained there with the kings of Persia. (Daniel 10)

I encourage those familiar with this account in Daniel to consider the possibility that this "prince of Persia" used to live on earth rather than being a fallen angel. Yes, in the *Parable of the Rich Man* there is the account of a wicked human going right to hell, but people go where their heart dictates. The rich man felt guilty of his crime of neglecting the poor and the only place his conscience could be consoled was in a pit in hell:

> 24 And he cried and said, Father Abraham, **have mercy on me,** and send Lazarus, that he may dip the tip of his finger in water, and cool my tongue; for I am tormented in this flame.
> 28 For **I have five brethren;** that he may testify unto them, lest they also come into this place of

torment. (Luke 16)

The wicked who, upon death, have no guilty conscience but are tied with all their hearts to an earthly pursuit will continue in that pursuit after death (unless there are contributing circumstances that will activate God to immediately consign them to hell). As far as I can tell, God does not care who does the tempting be it a fallen angel or self-assuming departed human.

My take away from this is that when Jesus judged 7 churches in the first chapters of The Revelation of John, though each church was doing some things right, they were also doing some things wrong, some were worse than others. Of course there were more than just 7 churches at the time and so it is believed that these 7 represent the most common pitfalls Christians have and we are meant to learn from their mistakes to avoid making the same. For example, Jesus told of one church that had left its "first love":

4 Nevertheless I have somewhat against thee, because **thou hast left thy first love.** (Revelation 2)

Of course everyone's first love after Jesus is spreading the *Good News* and witnessing its power to effect change in the lives of others. Instead of sharing that great news, the church at Ephesus was too busy playing church or "singing to the choir." So far as I know, Jesse does not reach out directly to the non-Believers but spends his time preaching to the choir and going from one church to another. And though he can make an audience laugh, the love of bringing non-Believers to Christ is ignored. With all that wealth, he could be spending his time and energy reaching those in need, which brings me to my one valid criticism that even his staunchest defender cannot ignore—the *Parable of the Sheep and Goats.*

Sheep & Goats

Jesus spoke most about the folly of being rich while others suffer. The following parable is a stern warning to the rich:

31 When the Son of man shall come in his glory, and all the holy angels with him, then shall he sit upon the throne of his glory:
32 And before him shall be gathered all nations: and he shall separate them one from another, as a shepherd divideth his sheep from the goats:
33 And he shall set the sheep on his right hand, but the goats on the left.
34 Then shall the King say unto them on his right hand, Come, ye blessed of my Father, inherit the kingdom prepared for you from the foundation of the world:
35 **For I was an hungred, and ye gave me meat: I was thirsty, and ye gave me drink: I was a stranger, and ye took me in:**
36 **Naked, and ye clothed me: I was sick, and ye visited me: I was in prison, and ye came unto me.**
37 Then shall the righteous answer

him, saying, Lord, when saw we thee an hungred, and fed thee? or thirsty, and gave thee drink?

38 When saw we thee a stranger, and took thee in? or naked, and clothed thee?

39 Or when saw we thee sick, or in prison, and came unto thee?

40 **And the King shall answer and say unto them, Verily I say unto you, Inasmuch as ye have done it unto one of the least of these my brethren, ye have done it unto me.**

41 Then shall he say also unto them on the left hand, Depart from me, ye cursed, into everlasting fire, prepared for the devil and his angels:

42 For I was an hungred, and ye gave me no meat: I was thirsty, and ye gave me no drink:

43 I was a stranger, and ye took me not in: naked, and ye clothed me not: sick, and in prison, and ye visited me not.

44 Then shall they also answer him, saying, Lord, when saw we thee an

hungred, or athirst, or a stranger, or naked, or sick, or in prison, and did not minister unto thee?

45 Then shall he answer them, saying, Verily I say unto you, **Inasmuch as ye did it not to one of the least of these, ye did it not to me.**

46 **And these shall go away into everlasting punishment: but the righteous into life eternal.** (Matthew 25)

We know that these many wealthy televangelists know this verse (and others like it) and yet they continue to "fleece the flock." What disturbs me most is their lack of fear for offending God.

Journey 18 - Land of the Master

Recently, Our Savior invited me to His homeland. What you are about to read are some of my experiences there, with Jesus as my guide. I had never been to the Holy Land, and I did not have a desire to go when I received Jesus' invitation. Because this was going to be a private tour, I did not go with a group. I went alone with the Master and the Holy Spirit as my guides.

With a very limited amount of time, I began to make preparations to travel when it suddenly occurred to me that

Jesus wanted me to go during the Passover/Easter season! Within one week, I had made travel arrangements, but still did not know where I would stay. My thoughts turned to Israel and Jerusalem, the place where Jesus spent most of His life. At least, that's what I had thought. However, He corrected my understanding and said Galilee is where He'd spent most of His life; that is where He wanted me to focus a good portion of my attention.

When I thought upon His correction, I realized that it was I who did not understand upon my first contemplation that Jerusalem was more a part of His ministry at the end of His life. In fact, if He were going to take me for a tour of His homeland, Jerusalem would be but a small part of it, with Galilee, including Nazareth, and Capernaum as the larger parts. I don't know that I will give a moment-by-moment account of what I did such as one would find in a travel log, but I will give whatever He wants with sufficient narration to tell the story.

What was the purpose of Jesus inviting me to His homeland? Was it because of His favor or did He have nothing better to do? That would be preposterous, as Jesus loves all of God's children and does not show favoritism (except when it comes to His Father). He does favor Our Father above all others, and He still does only that which His Father says to do.

So I would like to thank Our Father for His permission and for the accompaniment of the Savior, for the Holy Spirit, and the gifts that have been given me for the task. Having made that clarification, let me explain what the purpose of my trip was. It was not to make a chronicle of His life. What information we have today is limited in scope for a reason, as His brother James told me.

To focus on any particular area outside of His ministry would draw more attention to Himself and less on our Heavenly Father. Everything Jesus did was for the purpose of turning people to the Father. One of the hardest things I had to deal with during this trip (as in other spiritual journeys) was that of reference. Everything Jesus referenced for me was not within my framework of experience being an **English**-speaking **American** in the year **2004.**

How we Americans do things is so different from how they did things back then. To understand that element alone would have caused hours of translation, which we did not have. God always works within our limited frameworks. If I were a local Arab or Jew, I am sure the dialogue would have been much more interesting and of greater depth, to say the least. Many who go to the Holy Land go there with great expectation within the framework of **prophecy**. They read of the prophecies already fulfilled and the ones yet to be fulfilled, and that shapes the extent of their view.

Though I am aware of said prophetic frameworks, none of it was fresh in my mind at that time. I recalled only vague views of a Jewish temple to be built on the Temple Mount and a final battle in

Megiddo or Armageddon. Because I know our Savior as a person rather than a thing of history, I had some desire to know more of His personal background, like where He lived and where key Biblical events that pertained to Him took place.

I believe one can have an awareness of, or sensitivity to, historic spiritual imprints. But we can only understand what is within our scope of experience and our framework of allowance. Therefore, each person's interpretation may vary according to details, but not according to the place of the event. Being called to the Holy Land without time to prepare historical references was, I believe, Jesus' way of making sure I did not come with more preconceived notions than I already had. My framework was the love of God first and the glory of His presence; I do not hold those captive to any framework. If there is love, I will respect it, and where there is God's presence, I will acknowledge it.

Now on to the particulars of this

spiritual journey.

*Merchants outside Herod's Gate, which
continue on inside the old city.*

Anyone who has been to Jerusalem may know that it is a "tourist trap." This fact made it almost impossible to discern any historical truth. Combine that with the repetitions of those frameworks with great expectation, including both Jews and Christians, and it is nearly impossible to discern any element of the true prophetic there. That is, without God's assistance.

May I first say while it is fresh in my

mind and burning in my heart that Jesus lives, for I have seen Him many times, and He has seen me and revealed His glory to me; He has cleansed me of all my sins. His light forever changed me, and for that I owe Him all the praise and honor and glory that can be bestowed. And, I know He does all things in the will of Our Father, who also deserves all the praise and glory!

I thank you, Jesus, for doing it all. I thank you, Father, for the magnificence of it all. Your love is so deep and so wide, please help our unbelief and expand our limited belief systems. Remove all previous notions of what is supposed to happen as we compare it with what did happen, both the "why" and the "how." Father, please help me to tell it well and layer it well, for there are many things on different levels, and I pray I can coherently tell them all.

The key events commonly spoken of in the Bible have faithfully been preserved, and I am witness that they are real and bear my witness; herein you shall have them.

I arrived on **Good Friday**, an event that Latter-Day Saints do not recognize, whereas the Roman and Orthodox, the Protestant and Charismatics do mostly honor this tradition. It was early on Friday morning when Our Lord was outside the city walls suffering from the weight of compressions (i.e., a convergence of the past with the future) upon him. He knew that His time was near, but His disciples could not lend Him a hand, whether in knowing or by consoling. This is the loneliest feeling of all, when your best friends don't even know you are suffering!

Instead of looking due east from Jerusalem as the place Jesus often went, we need to look more southeast, for Jesus always had the city in his northern (NW) view. Around a slight hill can be viewed the place He and His disciples often went, away from the view of those in the city. That is important to keep in mind. Trees were also prevalent, not bare as the land is today.

Eastside view from Jerusalem looking further south than the Mount of Olives. Jesus often came and went between this first hill and the one behind it.

Jesus was staring from that southerly viewpoint toward Jerusalem when He had His first impression that things would not end well for Him in Jerusalem this time. That is the direction from which I, too, approached the city while walking late at night into the early hours of the morning. As I walked, I passed a Nomad who was sleeping just outside the old city walls, with his son and their camel in the field. Such is the view today with the old and the new side by side. I marveled at that.

I walked through the city, which had long, narrow streets, all made of stone, just like it was back then. But to see the real stone streets one must go to select archaeological spots. Eventually I came to a small group of people funneling out of one of the Orthodox churches on the "Via Dolorosa" or "Way of Sorrows," the alleged route Jesus bore His cross. I say *alleged*, for these streets have been remade many times over the years. Nevertheless, it was so late (or early in the morning) that the streets were vacant.

I stood and watched as priests and nuns aligned in procession, each bearing a cross and candle, with the leader carrying the largest cross. At this late hour, they all knew what they were doing and only slightly minded my observing them. Without anything being said, the Savior came and stood beside me and expressed His appreciation for what they were doing. For all throughout the day this time of year the city is polluted by merchants. At least here was a faithful group whom I felt were in a discipline of honoring the sacred. Whether only on Good Friday or every Friday I do not know, but Jesus respected their humble and disciplined efforts.

Their procession led silently out of the city wall from the Via Dolorosa, past St. Stephen's Gate, then down to the main road, past the grotto and into a convent. There the procession abruptly ended with nothing being said, and I was left to myself outside their walls in the dark.

The road entrance to Orson Hyde Garden is full of dumped garbage.

I walked on down the road, and to my surprise (after plowing through piles of rubbish in the dark) I came to a gate that read "Orson Hyde Foundation." Now that was a surprise! There I was on the Mount of Olives and here was something with which I was familiar. This entire park was dedicated by the "Orson Hyde Foundation of Salt Lake City." No mention of the church was on it, but there didn't need to be with the words "Salt Lake City" there. It was sadly obvious that others had tried to chip away the words "Salt Lake City" from the marker.

Near the entrance to the Orson Hyde Garden

Amazed as I was, I proceeded up the mountain in the still of the night enjoying the view of the old city and the Dome of the Rock as I went. I could tell many groups had been here, with highly educated views being given, but the presence of Our Lord was not there to any noticeable degree. I decided to sleep the first night there and to reflect upon the events in Jesus' life. For the LDS Church to have a spot on the Mount of Olives is awesome, but to think it is a spot Jesus frequented would be an error. That is not the view He often had of the city.

Early in the day I was able to view the Western Wall (or Wailing Wall) during that Passover season, which brought in large numbers of Jewish people from around the world. This brought forth fond memories of my mission when I was assigned to the Jewish people and learned the Jewish Discussions (yes, there are or were Jewish Discussions) and worked among their people. These visitors were all very neatly dressed—"a very beautiful and delightful people"—the men, women, and children. For them, Passover was a family affair, and the children of each family were content.

I was impressed once again, just as I was on my mission. I enjoyed attending synagogue then, and I was enjoying visiting the Wailing Wall now. I had stood back for a while to observe it all, but the glory of the Lord was not there in a large way. I could see that the effect of their efforts went no higher than the top of the wall itself, as if they believed their prayers were being limited by it.

I want to say here and now for those who have not read my title *Set God Free,* God is waiting—and I mean *waiting*—for these people to do something *new,* for they are so stagnant. Many churches are doing the same things and are glorying in their void of growth, which is a deep-seated cancer that needs to be stopped.

Sign off the main street with a smaller one on

the wall.

Later the following day I just had to go to the **Garden Tomb.** I'd heard so much about it over the years by Latter-Day Saints claiming this was the spot of Jesus' resurrection. I missed the special Good Friday service there at the Garden Tomb; nevertheless I still wanted to see it for myself. Actually, the less of a crowd the better it was for me to visit.

Garden Tomb entrance back from the road.

I entered the walled complex (it took me forever to find; it's kind of hidden with very small signs). Through the gate and on my left I beheld the glory of the

Lord permeating the whole area. As the Father had multiplied the robins for me in the glory of his presence (see *Day of the Robin*) so, too, were the birds multiplying in response to the Lord's presence. Indeed, the way the park is set truly reflects the pattern in which the glory of Our Lord radiated (and still radiates).

For example, the area overhead should be left open for the glory to radiate upward, interacting with the sun's rays. The terrain should be ascending from the tomb with all the chairs centered around it and facing the tomb. I could easily imagine how an undiscerning people could have set this garden up with large shading trees over the tomb blocking the upward radiance of glory, but no, this is *feng shui* at its finest. I noticed a number of people meditating in lounge chairs, just basking in God's light just as one would bask in the sun's light. Others were meditating upon the Word of God.

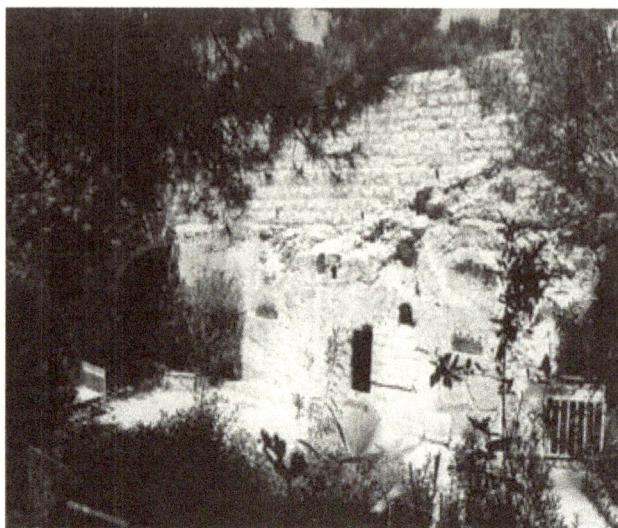

A traditional view of the tomb. The front has been repaired many times.

I found my own spot to observe the glory and noticed that the glory centers from about ten feet **in front** of the tomb rather than from within it. Even though the sign said it was closed for the day, I felt I needed to go inside, for if that was Christ's original tomb (how it was back then), I wanted to see what He saw as He came forth.

I approached one of the workers and asked why it was closed. She said, "It was not yet Sunday, and His body was still in the tomb," meaning the stone had not been rolled away yet (this was the only time of the year that they acknowledge the series of events and days associated with them).

I asked if they would make an exception because I was not going to be here another day, and permission was granted. Before I entered the tomb, I entered the center of the glory and noticed, again, that it was ten feet beyond the tomb so that when Jesus emerged, He would have first looked up and to His left (east). The glory still radiates up in an easterly way.

Standing in the glory looking eastward.

I went in the tomb but a residue of His presence was not on the inside of it. Thus

I believe the original tomb was somewhere around 10 feet out from its current location. On the far side of the Garden is a purported view of **Golgotha** (which is now a bus parking lot). It may be listed as Golgotha, but it is not the true Golgotha. I do know that Jesus was taken a significant distance (approximately 3 blocks) from where He was crucified to a quieter, more remote spot (modern-day Garden Tomb).

Some would like you to believe this was Golgotha, but it is not.

Mary mistook Jesus as the gardener, which means the tomb was in a garden.

They did not (at that time) torture and crucify people next to this garden. The place Jesus was brought to was, in relation to where He was murdered, **humble**, a **distance**, and **quiet**. Meaning it was not next to a busy road, merchants, nor a place used for death and suffering.

From there I rented a car and headed for Galilee, the place where Jesus grew up. I had heard that Mt. Tabor is where some claim Elijah ascended and Jesus was transfigured. If that were so, I definitely wanted to see it and confirm it. As I drove north out of Jerusalem, I saw a mountain just before Nazareth, where Jesus said He and His disciples had spent some time and where I would spend the night.

It is not until you go a little further north that you see Mt. Tabor off to the right, or east. While I did see a residue of the Lord's glory on it, I saw nothing on the current mount called Little Hermon. The next morning I drove into Nazareth.

Little Hermon as viewed from Nazareth looking south.

As you wind your way up the hill into Nazareth you come onto another busy town—another tourist trap—all bustling with merchants. I chose to stay away during day hours and waited until the coast was clear early in the morning. I also ventured out to the "Mount of the Precipice," which is the alleged place the citizens tried to throw Our Savior "down headlong" (Luke 4:29). As I looked around, Jesus pointed to the true place they tried to throw Him off, a place near where He often went in His early life.

True Mount of the Precipice as viewed from the traditional one.

Of all the areas in Nazareth, it is amazing this one small hill is still there, just a stone's throw from the town's center. I ventured over, found a small trail, and noticed the remnant of a monument of some kind near its top. I wondered if somebody else felt the significance of this hill and that is why they built something there?

An old monument at the top of Jesus' favorite hill as a child.

At the top of this hill is a large rock, the same rock Jesus saw more than two thousand years ago. Jesus told me that this is where He would come to pray. To His left (while looking east), He said, "I could see my mother's home, and to my right (south), I could see my Father's throne (temple in Jerusalem)," or at least that is how He viewed it back then. Further out along this hill is where they tried to toss Him off, it being closest to the town.

One large rock on Jesus' favorite hill looking south. Little Hermon is in the background.

You cannot, from this viewpoint, see Mt. Tabor. Mt. Tabor was nowhere in Jesus' sight, nor was it in line with most of His travels. The hill I was presently standing on, with this massive rock from more than two thousand years ago, I felt should be considered **holy ground.** Holy because this was where the young Jesus played, but also where He would pray and contemplate. It looks like some developments are encroaching this sacred land; I hope efforts are made to save it soon! A beautiful park could be made where the public could come like at the Garden Tomb in Jerusalem—away from the entire merchant hassle—to contemplate and pray.

On Jesus' favorite rock looking back at the old city of Nazareth.

When I was originally looking on the map of Galilee and the area around Nazareth, I noticed that Jesus was very fond of some areas and actually very bitter toward others. Even though Jesus was fully God and fully man, we fail to allow Him human feelings. The fully human side of Jesus did and does have strong feelings about certain people and events from His past. He has very hurtful feelings about a person associated with the area north of Nazareth.

Imagine if you will, knowing this earth is Your Father's throne. Imagine knowing that as His son, You actually own it but observe another claiming ownership and abusing it. That must have been one of the hardest things for Jesus to endure. So I went north out of Nazareth to see what it was that Jesus still had bitter feelings about. What I found was amazing. Off in the distance is **Zippori National Park.** This is the place where Herod Antipas reigned; it contained large structures that could be seen from all around, **including from Nazareth.**

You could stand at the edge of Nazareth's north edge and look down and see Antipas' elaborate dwelling place. This troubled the young Jesus for many years, and still to this day He holds bitter memories of this man, for His earthly father, Joseph, worked for him and was killed by him. This is the human side of Jesus I never knew before.

From Herod's palace in Zippori looking south to Nazareth on the hill.

Wanting to track Jesus' steps as best that I could, I returned to Nazareth and headed northeast, the way Jesus would go to the **Sea of Galilee**, which was the place for the rest of His ministry. As I traveled, things were pretty straightforward the way He went. Though His home became **Capernaum,** and we should have continued straight to that area, He commanded me to turn right and head for **Tiberias**. So I turned right as He commanded me (which was not the most direct route to Capernaum).

I asked Him why He commanded me to turn instead of going what was, according to my map, the most direct route?

He replied, "When you take the next turn, you will see why." Over the next turn, the **Sea of Galilee** suddenly appeared. He said that back then they almost always took the route closest to water:

Jesus' first view of the Sea of Galilee when approaching from Nazareth.

That view from the road, though not exactly what He saw, was very close. He said that this was the exciting view they had after a long day's travel, to come up over that ridge and see this body of water with that peculiar hill on the right and the lower one on the left. This is the view Jesus had. Though there are other views around the lake with more notable features, He said they were not present at His time.

Jesus' view departing the Sea of Galilee toward Nazareth.

Traveling north along the lake (for it is but a lake) I couldn't help but go for a swim. To swim in the same lake Jesus and His disciples swam in, fished in, and upon which Jesus walked would be a marvelous experience. With beaches all up and down the shore I did not know which one I should choose, then Jesus told me to take the next exit. Though I did not know why at the time, I soon discovered there was a museum containing a **two thousand-year-old fishing boat** that Jesus said would give me an idea of how some traveled on the lake.

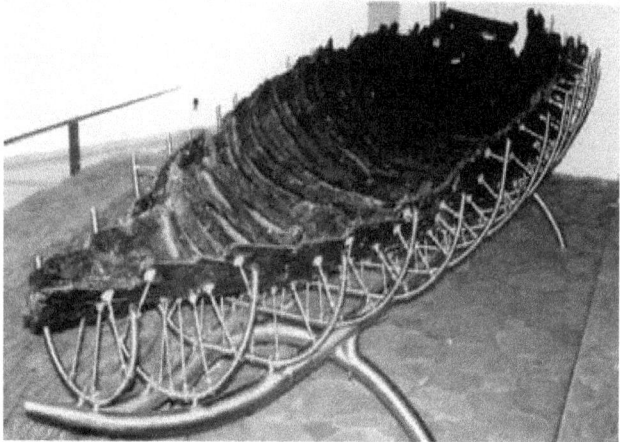

2000-year-old fishing boat like what Jesus and His disciples sailed in.

I thanked Jesus for the museum tour and for the swim, and then we continued heading north along the lake's shore. We stopped at several traditional places where Jesus allegedly performed miracles. Many of these Jesus did not feel were wrong, for He said it is good to have some place rather than no place to be remembered. And it pleased Him that they at least caused others to think upon those events in His life. Back in his day, the lake was much higher, and several of those purported "traditional locations" would have been under water at the time.

During this time my mind was also occupied with the spot of His transfiguration. I knew it was not Mt. Tabor as some teach. What about any of the other mountains around the lake? There was something on the east side which has a level ridge going along it that is fairly high up and resembles things during Jesus time, but I would not have time to learn what that was.

The location I did want to investigate was Mt. Hermon, which was significantly further north, a spot some claim is the same mountain used by other prophets. On my way there, I wanted to stop and see the **Jordan River** and **Bethsaida,** which was a town just north of the lake.

He took me back in time at that moment and I saw as they entered late at night and experienced the same raw, young feelings as Him at the beginning of His ministry of many unknowns. After performing a healing the next day His strength (in courage) grew. Though people cite when He turned water into wine as being his first miracle, that was a simple miracle, in a jolly environment among friends. This early experience that He was sharing with me was **entirely different.**

I next entered the **Jordan River Park,** which contained the archaeological site of Bethsaida, one of the towns Jesus first visited and performed miracles in. The riverside of the park was very busy with the locals, so I decided to stay away and first go to the archaeological side.

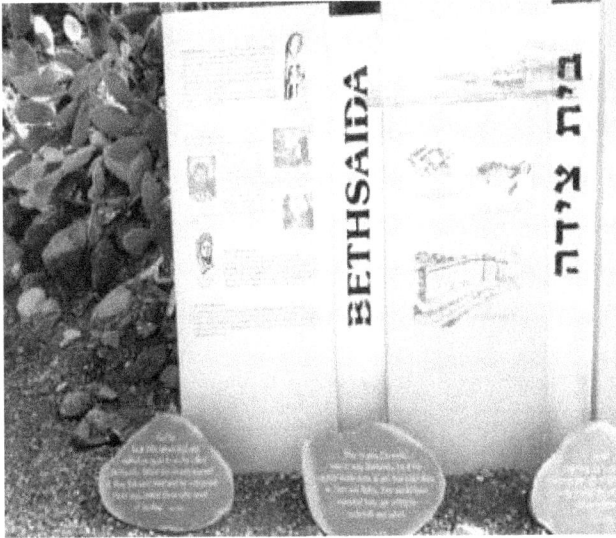

At the entrance of the trail to the Bethsaida archaeological site.

I was glad that I did. At the present time, it looks to be a fairly forsaken place, very dry, and nothing but rocks to see. I began the walking tour until it brought me to its furthermost part in a direction back toward the north side of the lake. Once at the end, I was exhausted from the heat and the lack of food and water, and I collapsed under the shade of a palm branch overhang. After I recovered, I stood to my feet and looked around. To my right (west, while facing south toward the lake), I saw along the top of an adjacent hill the glory of Our Lord radiating strongly upon it. This, Jesus said, was the spot of His **Transfiguration.**

Lookout point from the end of the trail in Bethsaida. The Sea of Galilee is straight ahead looking south with the true Mt. of Transfiguration on the right looking west.

Today there are not many trees on the mountain, but Jesus showed me how in His day there were; they looked to me like pine trees. There, near the top, Jesus left some of His disciples (Peter, James, and John) and went further up through the trees on His own. At this time Jesus had the **greatest expectation,** but His disciples were totally oblivious to what was about to take place.

Sea of Galilee on the left, the mount slowly rises to its highest point to the right with trees faintly seen along the top—the true Mt. of Transfiguration.

The experience was like people going to a particular spot expecting to make contact with extraterrestrials—that's how I would put it, because **that's exactly what I saw.** That was the exciting expectation Jesus was waiting for— contact from above by angels in **starships.** Recall how Elijah was taken up. This is how he would come again. Of course to be fair, today we would hardly call it a "chariot" but more like a celestial space vehicle of some sort. Jesus knew about this stuff and was excited to experience it firsthand.

The actual spaceship His disciples did not see, but they did see a light. Jesus went in and communed with Elijah and Moses (perhaps others, I could not see for the brightness of the light). When it left, Peter, James, and John saw the light from a distance, and then they saw Jesus shortly thereafter. I would have to say this was one of the most fantastic things I have ever seen, but it is not altogether foreign. Some of you might recall Jesse Duplantis was taken by a celestial vehicle to the Holy City. God uses mechanical vehicles at times and they can be clothed in His glory.

The sun was beginning to set and I wanted to see the top of that hill! I wanted to bathe in the glory where Jesus was transfigured. Not sure what I would find by car or if I should hike it from where I was, I was determined to get to it, by one way or another. To my surprise, I found a road that went up to where a small, gated community exists. I was able to go through the gate and find my way to the top.

Not sure where the exact top was amidst the homes, all of a sudden I entered the glory of Our Lord, and I knew it had to be close. I turned on the next street to find a great view of the lake and the surrounding area, including the Jordan River. It was beautiful! But I wanted to go to the exact spot with the four palm trees I saw from down below.

I drove just over the top of the hill onto its east side and there they were, next to a single white house on the exact spot. I thought to myself, 'These are the luckiest people in the whole world, to live in that historical glory 24/7! I wondered if they felt the beauty of the location? I wonder if any of the people there know how really special it is? It is more than just a great view; it is **historical** and **sacred**.

View of the Sea of Galilee from the true Mt. of Transfiguration.

I wanted to sleep there for the night in the presence of the glory of Our Lord, but Jesus told me to return to Jerusalem. I responded, "I just came from there, and it is such a long drive in the night, and there is more I want to see here." Then Jesus commanded me to return, so my journey in Galilee abruptly ended. Jesus wanted me to be there for the early morning Easter service back at the Garden Tomb. I took a few more pictures then headed south.

I drove all night into the early morning

hours and arrived outside the Garden Tomb where I slept for a few hours in the car. Around 5:30 I noticed people arriving for the 6:30 service. Since I had not eaten in two days, I thought I should go and find some nourishment before a long and emotionally exhausting service. I went to find food and when I returned there was a rather large crowd outside the Garden Tomb, so I forfeited the food once again for the food of the Spirit and joined the crowd.

It became clear that from all over the world thousands of people had come to celebrate one of the most sacred events in one of the most important spots. Praise God for the respect they all had! I was going to experience firsthand that little Garden Tomb secret!!

I received an anointing of the Holy Spirit there like no other. I am sure others did, too. The service was a combination of prayers and praise led by the worship group King of Kings. If only the LDS could see how true believers praise, maybe they would try doing the same.

From all over the world, people of all creeds, tongues, and denominations sang as one. Some spoke in tongues, but most were reserved. Others, like me, were just overcome by tears of emotion that threatened to overwhelm the mortal frame of my soul. I say if the people did not praise, the rocks would have burst forth in anthems of praise, so strong was the glory of Our Lord!

I will never forget that day of fellowshipping with the saints of God, of singing praises in honor of our King. Thanks be to those who found and have preserved that Garden Tomb so that we have it today; definitely a worthy cause to support, for many come to know the Lord there. Oh God, help us to know Your Love, so we know when we have it and when we don't.

I testify before all men that these things are true, that Jesus did rise from the dead and yet it was done not with a shaking and a big bang, but gentle, as a feather that falls to the floor unnoticed. Death and hell were stopped, and quite naturally Our Lord emerged. Jesus told me He has respected the efforts of what people do there for a long time, and it is a fine example of what God's love is all about. I don't believe this was a special service, for they have **always** been special, and what I will reveal now is what I have been commanded by Almighty God to tell.

You cannot receive the complete love of God, a true testimony of Our Lord, without receiving the stewardship that comes with it. Peter did not have this testimony at first. He had the "flesh and blood hath not revealed it unto thee" (Matt 16:17) testimony that is deniable under threat or coercion with which he had received and denied Our Lord. The testimony he later received of the **risen** Lord was different, and it is undeniable under any circumstance.

If you want to meet the risen Lord in person, be prepared to die for it. Do not seek that which under threat or duress you would not **clearly** and **presently** be willing to die for. I, who have been under the threat of Arabs and Jews, can testify that you must be willing to die for what you know, otherwise do not seek it. It took the good blood of many apostles and elders, prophets and others to bring about the good we have today, and we should not suppose it will not cost more blood to bring about more good.

If the Lord would ask me to give my life today I would do it, for such is the testimony I have been given and I can clearly say as Paul of old, "to be absent from the body (is) to be present with the Lord." (2 Cor 5:8) He did not mean as soon as anyone dies they are instantly with God. That may be comforting for grieving parents, spouses, or children, but it is not what Saul meant. I testify he said that because he saw the risen Lord, and the glory of His presence was revealed to him. After experiencing that, he could hunger for nothing other than that glory —that passes all understanding. Therefore, to be absent from the body, i.e., death through martyrdom, would be great, for his soul would be free to return home.

Isn't it wonderful to know when you are pleasing the Lord by the presence of His Holy Spirit?! Isn't it blessed to have the accompaniment of angels or the ministry of Jesus Himself?! But such things come at a cost. Do not pursue the call of prophets if you are not currently willing to give your life for it all. That's what our Father once said, and though I believe there are but a few willing to become prophets, those few must know these words, so they can know how to pray in the end.

I thank you for that word, dear Father, and pray that You will bless all who hear it.

That being my last day in Israel, I wanted to make the most of it and see a couple more things. From there I wanted to see the famous Dome of the Rock, so I made my way over, avoiding the inner merchant streets. I entered Stephen's Gate and immediately turned left toward the Dome of the Rock. As I did so, I entered a courtyard where children and others pass through on their way to school and to the mosque.

El Ghazali Square, the true place Jesus was condemned to die.

I stopped suddenly when the Lord said to me, "This is where I was condemned." I could not believe what He said. I was not ready to hear that! I stood amazed. Though the stone tiles were newer, nothing had been built over the spot. Here is where Our Lord was condemned to die. I wept bitterly over that spot and saw what our Father saw as He looked down upon it. Here, as in Nazareth, Jesus has bitter memories of these things.

I had just come from extreme joy at the

Garden Tomb, to extreme anger in this courtyard currently being used by children and others to go to mosque and to school—totally ignorant of its history. It is called El Ghazali Square, and though I don't know if the exact measurements reflect those of Jesus' time, the current square and the space above it are part of the original square where Jesus' fate was sealed, and He came to know within Himself that there was no hope for His release (Matt 27:27).

Upon looking at the maps I noticed that the first station on the Via Dolorosa (the alleged way of sorrows) through which Jesus traveled is in the courtyard of Omariye College, which is adjacent to this courtyard (they are separated by a small parking lot). I can only assume that back then the courtyard was much larger and covered all or nearly all of the area.

Jesus will not budge on this, and I testify that if you enter St. Stephen's Gate, turn left, walk fifty feet and look to your right (west) into the El Ghazali Square, you are looking into the space where

Jesus was condemned. And it was here, the final confronting spot, that He realized his fate was sealed, and this He retains memories of and manifests great anger for (which I will explain more on later).

From here I did find the one entrance to the Dome of the Rock over by the Wailing Wall. As I walked across the Temple Mount toward the Dome of the Rock, the Lord said to me, "You are now walking where David walked." I took this to mean that historically David had ownership of the Temple Mount, and I look forward to learning more about that.

I was not able to gain entrance to the Dome of the Rock or the El-Aqsa Mosque, and did not feel comfortable bribing the doorman as others suggested, so I left. It is an interesting thing to be Muslim and feel you are on "top of the world," having defeated your enemies, with the Jews praying to the side of an old wall **below** you. I say, that is a very telling thing indeed!

From there I went to the new archaeological site near the southeast corner of the temple, which is near the entrance to the Dome of the Rock and the Western Wall. Here they have uncovered many things dating back to the time of Jesus. As I walked around, the steps leading from the old Hulda Gates on the east side of the Temple Mount where people used to exit the temple, Jesus said, are original and that He actually walked on, sat upon, and taught the people there, on those very steps. I noticed that most had new stones added to them, but a few of the original were still exposed, having been preserved for thousands of years under dirt.

Original steps Jesus said he walked on, sat on, and taught on outside the Hulda Gates.

By this time I was exhausted from all the walking, lack of food, and dehydration, so we agreed it was time to go. The Jewish people were still arriving by the busloads and heading to pay homage at the Western Wall. A nice and delightful people, as I said to myself once more. This was truly a wonderful place that can accurately take you back in time more than **two thousand years** ago to capture how it was at the time of Christ. Perhaps even the mannerisms of the people are much the same, with their servitude to structures as their pathway to God.

One thing Jesus showed me the night I drove in from Bethsaida as I was approaching the city from the east (from the Dead Sea and Jericho) was the night of his **final** ascension, in the very city that killed him. Now I don't know exactly where that ascension took place, for He was far above it, but I saw how Jesus did bend our dimension into Heaven's. If you want to know what it looked like, first think in terms of something ancient, then imagine two layers or masks (as in photoshop) across the sky. Now place those two masks like an overlay in front of the Dome of the Rock and the city looking from the east.

The top layer is the celestial one, the bottom layer is our denser, earthly one. Now, recall that there is no space or time in the spiritual world as we now know it. So when the two dimensions merge, time is going to be affected on our end. There will be a momentary shift in our time. Then as Jesus merges into the heavenly dimension, it will appear as if He is standing in the lower layer and ascending into the heavenly. It's like an upside down funnel.

The reason Jesus showed me this was because He wanted me to understand one of the reasons for their being a distinct heavenly, portal-like feeling in the Holy Land.

Additional Notes

I was appalled at the filthiness of some of the sites, and Jesus said, "It is hard to take pride in something you do not believe in. Nevertheless, they won't cut off the hand that feeds them—tourists."

Upon walking on the true hill they tried to throw Jesus off in Nazareth, the Father said, "They tried to hurt my son."

Jesus:

"Jerusalem for me was pitted God against man. Man because he wouldn't listen, and God because He would not hear their prayers. Vain works never get you to Heaven. Only through My grace that was given. Islam, Buddhism, and other religions require servitude to structures that go on living, but in the end, they are of no use, having no power in removing sin or in seeing God's face as Moses did."

"I especially enjoyed the company of men. My stepfather had many brothers, and they had aunts and uncles."

"I had every intention of coming off triumphant and delivering the people from oppression and sin. By throwing off their separation by sin, they could have staved off oppression from Rome."

Jesus said this because I noticed he is still very much bothered by what Herod Antipas and Pilate did. Even Pilate's wife had a dream to warn her husband **NOT to harm Jesus** (Matt 27:19). Jesus said:

"The will of God was halted, and I was hung on a cross as a common thief, and yet I had done nothing wrong."

"There are other ways I could have spilt my blood; it did not have to be that way. It bothers Me to this day that on God's earth, man is not His footstool but act like kings ruling contrary to Me, the King of Kings!"

"I tried to stem the tide of the Roman invasion. There are many kingdoms, not just one. Rome is one, Islam another. They all have their rulers."

Jesus came to break the bands of death and hell. Hell, by committing no sin. Death, by rising from the dead. That was for all people, for all periods of time, and not just the Jewish people.

"Just as animal sacrifice was purely meant to be symbolic so, too, was my death meant to be symbolic, and the method was a nonissue."

"Jews/Christians think of Isaiah and Joseph as guardians of prophecy, but the greatest truth is I am able to **commute prophecy** to whatever way suits me; if not, then I am not God."

"The great truth is I did not even have to be born like this. I could have come and gone, quietly fulfilling God's law, if man had only decided as a whole to return home. Many did, as you know, and it could have been everyone."

"No atonement was necessary for Enoch to prevail! I could have still gone to hell, delivered the prisoners, and shown them the way home."

"The illusion is that I have come to save man from their sins. I can no more do that than I could make a cow sing with his bell. The two go together, but are not necessarily dependent on each another."

"Through choice of action, man creates a life of his own. A simple life confession cannot replay his whole life in a new way. He is still holding the causes for the actions of sin. To admit those actions is a beginning, but it certainly is not the ending."

"In order to weed out sin, a man must turn his soil, furbish it into new ground that is unsuitable for weeds or sin to grow in. A person must create new soil. Of course the touch of my love does wonders in providing them with direction. And that is all anybody can do: find the light and build their terrain so that it is conducive to it."

"They labor every day building structures to suit them. If they would only build suitable structures compatible with the Light, My Light would always be with them [communities, not church]."

"Between man's habits and his support structures, man is fully capable of taking control of his life just like Adam, Seth, Enoch, and others did."

"My coming was purposed for returning God's children back to the life they once had; they had gotten so far off track I had to come. Else, they would have stayed just as they were, and now two thousand years later, you can see those who chose against me **have remained the same**."

"My coming was necessary because for two thousand years my people were still no further."

"God chose the time I would break death and hell to coincide with the needs of His people. I could have come earlier; I could have come later. But with Rome becoming a great power, I tried to stem their tide."

"Right now it seems we are much further because there are so many Christians in the world. But if you look at their lifestyles, you will notice they have substituted one set of structures for another."

"Unless you are developing as a

person by cultivating good soil, all the outward configurations won't mean a thing, whether you recognize Me as God or not."

"The Buddhist nations advance further after death because their soil is more fertile. With simple instructions they are able to go further." (He is referring to progress in the spirit world.) Christians, however, though they know My words of instructions, have not fertilized their soil with them. It takes them a lot longer to go further (in the spirit world)."

"In the end, it is not whether you know your Lord or have confessed His words, but whether your soil is fertile. Enoch's soil was so fertile he could go straight home without a Savior. This point should commend my people to focus more on the soil of their souls than anything else. Only **you** can control your destiny. No one for you, no one against you. You can recite prayers, offer alms, perform long pilgrimages, but if the condition of your soil is cold, I can't help you."

"God has never condemned you. That is an old tale made to prevent you from your greatness."

"Tie that to justification by your works and you have a solution to keep you going to church."

"Sainthood is not the same as church-hood. Penance is not godhood. When I said unto you to be 'perfect,' this means to be perfectly furnished/developed. Read the Sermon on the Mount. It is not instruction for the magical removal of bad character, but recommendations on how to till the soil to make it conducive to God's light. It is all about the Sermon on the Mount, My Atonement aside."

"I could have done much more good, made the transition easier for my people, if Pilate had listened to his wife. **That proposition is an option that all people should**

consider. If I had lived a long life and died of old age, would it have mattered? I would have still had to separate from my Father, and chosen Him and His will over the people, and lay my life down and pick it up again. My task was to conquer death and sin. Period."

"And if My teachings had succeeded, My people would not be bound to church structures, and their acceptance of the Sermon on the Mount as their master would have prevailed."

"My message is for all traditions where people serve structures at the expense of self-development."

"Because I was not able to fully succeed with My people, the chances of Me succeeding with other traditions were even harder."

"The sooner My own people can free themselves of this corruption and claim the rights that they innately have—without justification—the sooner God's children can get to Heaven."

My Thoughts

At this point I only want to draw attention to two things. First, the Mosaic law was a lower or lesser law. It was one given to a rebellious and disobedient people. Recall that when Moses went up on the mountain to receive the law of God for the children of Israel, he came back and destroyed them after seeing their rebellion.

That higher law is what Enoch accessed, and it got him into Heaven. It had nothing to do with the sacrifices of God's precious animals. That was a lower law, **not a permanent law**, just like divorce is a lower law, but not the original one. Today, we should be able to understand the differences and not be compelled to use a lower law as God's foundational law for man.

The second point is, Jesus could have done much more than He did. God does not prophesy doom; they are alternatives

His prophets make the people aware of, but in no certain terms are we meant to fulfill them. We as Christians must learn this one thing: God wants us to do all that we can do, and He continually wants us to perform **new** things, or progress will never come.

All progress found itself pitted against the Church, for the Church was locked into prophecies of **unchanging doom.** Prophecies are warnings of what will happen **if** we do not change. They are not to be used as roadmaps to follow, except the good ones that prophesy our potential.

Had Pilate listened to his wife's dream, Jesus would have lived. That is a spiritual truth I am yet to hear anyone point out. Jesus felt His time was cut short. He wanted to do more, and could have done more as He said by changing people's servitude to structure, but He could not do it by replacing Himself with their existing one.

He came to save people from their sins —their own separation from their Creator

—by serving lifeless structures that cannot save. Jesus spilt his blood in the Garden of Gethsemane when he **literally sweat blood**. He never had to be scourged, yet alone crucified. Those were worst-case scenarios/prophecies that Jesus never hoped for. We should not hope for worst-case scenarios either. Right now this world could turn into a garden paradise because the Christians outnumber other religions. The fact that it currently is not, is proof we are being misled regarding how God acts and the purpose prophecy is to perform.

I testify that Jesus taught me and showed me this. The sooner we wake up to the opportunities given us, the sooner we will take ownership of it. The sooner we take ownership of this world, the sooner we can **commute all prophecies** and turn this world into a living paradise! Though I am far too close to this experience now, I do want to express gratitude to everyone who made this journey possible: our Father, the Savior, my many friends and family, and **especially my wife Tammy.**

To God be all the glory,

Amen.

Jordan River in Bethsaida before entering the Sea of Galilee.

Journey 19 - Teacher of the Master

Parthenon

Introduction

Writing another title as I have been called by God to do, I must say that it is not God leading me as a robot that I do these things, but it is my heart that does them. For if I never sought for peace that only God could give, I would have never found Him. But find Him I did, and find peace I did also. It has been that longing for the peace that only God can give that has pushed me ever on in pursuit of His glory.

147

Upon receiving a direct manifestation of His glory and having gained firsthand knowledge of His love for all people, I know that **whatever divides us is not good for us,** for we are all God's children and are all the same, yet we do not treat each other like we are. These differences and the dogmas that divide us have caused me great pain. Knowing that God is the Father of us all and knowing of His love for all His children, it is unbearable to affirm anything as being sanctioned from Him that causes divisions, and by that I mean religion.

I don't know that others can appreciate that statement, but it is true and has only come from communing with Him directly. You will notice that it is often reported from beyond the grave that when you first cross over, if you meet your maker, you will not be asked what religion you joined. What you will be asked is what you learned and what you did with your time on earth. Even when Jesus was upon the earth, He did not start a church, but He did start an **educational program** that taught people about Him and His Father, our heavenly Father.

Most of Jesus' teachings can be found in the Sermon on the Mount, which we can use as a guide for happy living, both in this life and the life to come. Jesus as half-God had perfect sight that allowed him to see other dimensions of spirit, and He was keenly aware of the impact our actions have. Confessions of faith are nice outward professions, but if there is no transfer to the inner dimension, they are of little worth. The people in Jesus' day had plenty of outward confessions of faith, but not much was transferring inward.

This, Jesus called, **servitude to structure** at the expense of our inner or higher self and at the expense of our relationship to the Father. It is those who came after Him who set up churches that grew into structures that drew power unto themselves. Originally, apostles taught the resurrection of Christ, prophets revealed the will of God, and elders were in charge of organizing the local **educational efforts**. Teachers taught, and deacons assisted. It was all about **education**.

The New Testament refers to people meeting in their homes and amphitheaters, but the idea of physically building a church never occurred to them. Those were the later additions of man.

Right now, imagine if you will what God and angels see as they look down on the earth. They see farmland sectionalized and precisely divided. Then as they look over our cities they see the people sectionalized, **precisely divided by their churches.** For every physical church structure erected there is a precise division of the people. Yet each church feels certain that they are doing God's will.

One must ask, "How is sectionalizing the people doing God's work?" Are we not all God's children? **How can anything that brings division be approved by God?** We must recall that this holy mess called Christianity came *after* the holy mess called Judaism. Why do I say *mess*? Look at the fruits of the Christian world—

and yes, Christianity has been the largest religion on earth for more than a thousand years. Before then, we had the Jewish nation, which was so rebellious that Moses—not God—brought in hundreds of lower laws.

Moses saw fit to destroy God's teachings on the first tablets, and we want to somehow legitimize his actions and claim they were from God? The first thing the Jewish people need to do is throw out the laws of Moses and begin afresh by trying to figure out what was on those original tablets written by God! And the first thing Christians need to do is close down all their churches or convert them into schools or community centers, so they can begin participating in God's church—**The Church of Everyone** —and truly make a difference!

Do we really need churches to tell us to do what indigenous peoples have known for centuries: to love our neighbor as ourselves? Jesus said to hang all the laws on that one principle, and yet somehow we overlook that message for the message of eternal judgment and inherent sin. While each church is going about doing their own thing, they have ostracized themselves from the world, which is made up of God's children. What is the greater sin? Only those who truly know God will be able to figure that out.

Well I have figured it out, but it took me awhile, for I love the churches, and would never have thought to look beyond them. But we must rise above them if we are going to succeed in arriving at our destiny as humanity. Yes, there is a divine destiny for all of us, not just in death, but in life, and God has been doing His level best to advance **all** of us, at the same time, so that all may move beyond this present mortal toil.

Elijah and Enoch moved on, and we are destined to move on, too—to a new Heaven and a new earth, and God wants the whole world to do it! The Christian churches know most about this new earth, and yet they stand by **waiting** for it to happen, like sideline spectators. The truth is, **God** is the one standing by waiting for **us** to do something. If all Christians stopped serving their individual structures and started serving each other, this world would soon become a garden paradise.

To get there will be a step-by-step approach, beginning with where we presently stand. Many of my writings have been designed to do just that over the years, and my future titles will detail further plans that can accommodate everyone. The most important point in this plan is to lay the philosophical groundwork first, so all can understand it. What I am going to share next is the basis for that framework, and I am going to give it the same way that Jesus received it, for Jesus was taught and ministered to by many others, not just Elijah and Moses.

There were angels and teachers, all in accordance with God's pattern of allowing each person to carry on with whatever work they developed in life. Each person's work does follow them, and the work Jesus was most challenged by was the desire of people to serve structures rather than each other. That was the challenge in His day, and that challenge remains for us now.

The expert for this type of work, which also followed him into the next life, was **Socrates**. Socrates himself was challenged by a widespread servitude to structure: the Greek gods! Nothing could have been more difficult for him to combat. But he did. The methods he used are scarcely known, but there are enough of them to show us how. Before I share my experiences with Socrates, I want to address man's view of God first.

No structure. No filter.

Man's View of God

You have to experience God to know Him, yet we have come here to experience life— a seeming paradox, I know.

Here are some observations:

1. Are we meant to experience God

while in this life?

If we assume God to be nonhuman then it can become confusing. Man has invented many gods to accommodate his feelings of belonging not just physically to this earth, but cosmically to the universe.

2. Man's desire to belong has been made to serve different purposes over the ages of time, as is shown in the histories of different people

That longing among all cultures separated from one another is evidence that man is a part of something greater than himself—not necessarily of this earth —and beyond his immediate reach— being cosmically connected.

3. Man gets confused only when he assumes the Creator to be other than human

The greatest discovery since Adam is that man is/has been made in the image of man, and that God is human, albeit a superhuman. It is that superhuman quality we have all inherited that drives man to better himself and is the self-regulating part by which we measure ourselves.

4. It is only when man assigns the Creator elements that are not like His own that man acts adversely or unjustly

Even if God is left out of the equation and man treats singly and directly his fellowman as he would like to be treated, that is closer to the truth and more humane than any dogma that he has before created, including Greek or Egyptian gods, state-run communism, or Christianity.

We should not have to believe in a god in order to treat each other humanely. But if we are going to believe in God, we should believe in Him correctly; the correct way is humanely. For even a cosmic god would show no favoritism over humans, as they would all appear the same to him. Even the greatest human would still appear but a mere human; therefore, it would not serve the god's purpose to divide the people in any way that would cause them to harm others.

5. A religion that is humane or no religion at all

Not Judaism, Islam, Christianity, or Mormon. They all teach elitism and favoritism while trying to teach others how to conduct their life.

6. If your god is not human, keep God out of it

Jesus' message could have been well received if his physical proof that God was human came into it. Instead, people did not hear it, so they did not treat people humanely. Jesus' teachings on humanity were awesome, but somehow they got overshadowed by religious structures—of which He established none. Teachers and witnesses, yes; but structures, no. Structures came later as people tried to control and give order to their movement the only way they knew how—by setting up structures.

7. How to break the power of Rome

Fascinating, to break the Roman structure, God first had to deliver Peter and Saul from their own religious

structures before sending them to Rome.
Jesus first delivered them from serving
religious structure, so that they could be
sent to Rome as his educated
ambassadors.

Keep these seven points in mind as you
go through this title.

Socrates (469-399 BC)

Socrates was killed as was Jesus for not
abiding by the structures of his day. Most
people know Socrates through the study
of philosophy, but Socrates was an
honorable man, not just a philosopher.
Most book authors primarily look at the
philosophy of Socrates, noting his piety as
only secondary. I would like to turn that
around, for even philosophy hints of
structure, and Socrates himself said he
served no theory or formula, but had as
his primary goal the pursuit of truth.

His approach wasn't filtered through
some structure, or philosophy, though at
times he applied different formulas to test
people's theories. His method of

questioning may be looked at as a philosopher philosophizing, but Socrates actually claimed to have no philosophy other than the pursuit of truth. Later writers and followers of Socrates did develop structures and filters by which they applied it to an original discourse by Socrates, but these were of their own making and not his (see Plato's *Republic*).

Because we have a variety of writers talking about Socrates through confirmed contemporary sources, it does not take mystical historical lenses to view his character or his reasons for dying. What will take some time applying is the fact that Jesus was personally tutored by Socrates and strengthened by him as he approached death. Actually it is not that large of a step to connect the two considering how God allowed two others —Elijah and Moses—to tutor Jesus. No doubt they tutored Jesus on items they were experienced in (not death), and Socrates was experienced in the free-will submission of death.

That is what Socrates did when he

freely drank the cup of hemlock, though he could have been rescued from it. And this is what Jesus had to do when he drank from the cup that the Father gave Him, even though He could have been rescued from it. The second reason Socrates tutored Jesus was because they were both facing widespread, blind servitude to structures that had taken on a life of their own, leaving the people powerless and alienating them from God.

For Jesus it was the Jewish people who had been serving a structure set up since Moses. With hundreds of laws to abide by, the Jewish people were quite busy serving that structure with nothing new to show for it, unless of course some personal meaning could be imagined, as with the Kabala. With Socrates, the people of Greece and Athens were equally serving structure, with their servitude not just to one god, but to many gods, and the people were not any better for it.

You can hear Jesus now:

Woe unto you scribes and Pharisees, hypocrites! For ye pay tithe of mint and anise and cumin, and have omitted the weightier matters of the law, judgment, mercy, and faith: these ought ye to have done, and not to leave the other undone (Matt 23:23).

And you can hear Socrates proclaim the exact same message to his people:

Are you not ashamed that you give your attention to acquiring as much money as possible, and similarly with reputation and honor, and give no attention or thought to truth and understanding and the perfection of your soul (*Apology*, 29d).

These two prophets—for rightly they were—came to each of their people with a higher view of how things were to be, and tried to save mankind from the path they were on, to try and get them to see from higher ground what was around them. Jesus came as the literal son of God and was blessed from birth to have a higher view of what was true. We read that during His ministry he was filled with the Spirit of God as He worked:

And Jesus being filled of the Holy Ghost returned from Jordan, and was led by the Spirit (Luke 4:1).

So, too, was Socrates blessed from birth to be led by the Spirit of God:

I am subject to a divine or supernatural experience, which Meletus saw fit to travesty in his indictment. It began in my early childhood—a sort of voice which comes to me (*Apology*, 31d).

This duty which I have accepted, as I said, in obedience to God's commands given in oracles and dreams and in every way that any other divine dispensation has ever impressed a duty upon man (*Apology*, 33c).

Having received those blessings from God to be able to have higher sight, each knew that blindly serving structure was as bad as blindly serving anything other than God.

Jesus said:

> Ye are the salt of the earth: but if the salt have lost his savour, wherewith shall it be salted? It is henceforth good for nothing, but to be cast out, and to be trodden under foot of men (Matt 5:13).

Socrates also chastised those who wasted their time on earth not hurting anybody but not going forward either:

> I suppose that the happiest people, and those who reach the best destination, are the ones who have cultivated the goodness of an ordinary citizen, so-called "temperance" and "justice," which is acquired by habit and practice, without the help of philosophy and reason.

How are these the happiest?

Because they will probably pass into some other kind of social and disciplined creature like bees, wasps, and ants (*Phaedo*, 82b).

Peter did tell us of a better place in the next life, even a place with God if we were diligent in this life.

> Whereby are given unto us exceeding great and precious promises: that by these ye might be partakers of the divine nature, having escaped the corruption that is in the world through lust. (2 Peter 1:4).

Socrates likewise believed in a level of celestial living and put it this way:

> **No soul which has not practiced philosophy, and is not absolutely pure when it leaves the body, may attain to the divine nature that is only for the lover of learning** (*Phaedo*, 82c).

And of course, for those at the other end of the spectrum, who neither applied themselves decently in or toward the divine order, there is a separate place for them as well. In the parable of the rich man, Jesus described a rich man in hell being separated from the others by a gulf (Luke 16:23, 26). Socrates imagined these same people being "compelled to wander about these places as a punishment for their bad conduct in the past" (*Phaedo*, 81d).

In any case, both Jesus and Socrates understood that there were three classes of people. To put it more succinctly, Paul said he went to the "third Heaven" (2 Cor 12:2) and described three groups in the resurrection (1 Cor 15:40). Socrates described the three classes on earth this way:

> There are not many very good or very bad people, but the greatest majority are somewhere between the two (*Phaedo*, 90a).

For the largest group, these are those

who are thoughtlessly participating in or giving service to structures. To believe in something **uncritically** Socrates termed *misology*. The results of which he said would be that the person would end up unwilling to believe in anybody (*misanthropy*). I would add for those serving religious structures, the result will be they will end up unwilling to believe in God at all (*misotheism*).

> Misanthropy is induced by believing in somebody quite uncritically. You assume that a person [or structure] is absolutely truthful and sincere and reliable, and a little later you find that he is shoddy and unreliable. The same thing happens again. After repeated disappointments at the hands of the very people who might be supposed to be your nearest and most intimate friends, constant irritation finally makes you dislike everybody and suppose that there is no sincerity to be found anywhere (*Phaedo*, 89d-e).

The same is true for those who go to church believing it is truthfully "God on earth," able to secure one's eternal salvation just so long as they serve, only in the end to find it leaves them feeling absolutely empty, wondering what to do. Some will fly as it were from that structure only to land on another, and possibly yet another, only to come to the end of their life wanting to run from them all and anything having to do with religion at all. This has been the fate of many men and women who have spent their life serving church as structures.

To avoid this situation, Socrates has given us the "Philosopher's Solution." Though I wish there were a better word to use then "Philosopher," you, like me, will in the end marvel at it.

The Philosopher's Solution

Stoa of Attalos

I traveled all the way to Greece at the request of one man—Jesus Christ. Upon an earlier tour of the Holy Land with Jesus as my guide, I happened to notice that while He was alive, He, too, had a guide. Soon it became apparent during my travels that there weren't just two of us on this trip, but three.

It wasn't long after I had written of my experiences in the Holy Land and had sent the manuscript out that I had great doubt that that title would be the end of it. Certainly Jesus brought clarification to many things, yet He was working within a limited framework in His day and with a limited amount of time. Today we find many in the same place as when Jesus was alive (Jews), but there are plenty of others who have gone on in even wider frameworks (Christians, Mormons, Pentecostal, etc.) and how to satisfy all of them was my task.

With that Jesus introduced me to His guide and good friend, Socrates, a man who lived and died well just as Jesus had. I was invited by Him to Socrates' homeland. I had never been to Greece, and the thought of going there was a bit overwhelming. Nevertheless, I mustered all my strength and did as I was commanded. Just as it was for me in the Holy Land, I discovered claims that were not accurate and things that are not known. Most of all, I discovered the terrain both physically and spiritually where it all began with this great man, Socrates, "a gift from the gods" some said, and I would add—a gift from the *One and Only True God*. Today we have many of Socrates' words, and they have been preserved to serve many different purposes, plus the one I am grateful to share next. Socrates took me to the island *Aegina*, through *Athens*, and to *Olympia*. He opened the eyes of my understanding and taught me many things (shared next).

Trapped in Structure

It is an inevitable fact that every soul who enters this earthly sphere will be brought up serving structures, but we are to escape from those structures and rise above them. Jesus put it this way:

> A man must be born again (John 3:3; see also 1 Peter 1:23).

Socrates likewise knew about this and spoke of it but not within the confines of a religious structure:

> Every seeker after wisdom knows that up to the time when philosophy takes it over, his soul is a helpless prisoner, chained hand and foot in the body, compelled to view reality not directly but only through its prison bars, and

wallowing in utter ignorance (*Phaedo*, 82e).

To many, the prison bars are the confines of established structures and limited frameworks that serve to shackle the mind. Where there is structure, there is lack of understanding, requiring no wisdom. All the learning has already been done; all one needs to do is follow. This is the dilemma that people of all generations have been faced with, whether political, mythological, or religious. **Whatever will require your service without the need of critical thinking will ensnare you, bind you, and blind you.**

Wisdom Is the Separator

Or as Socrates put it:

Wisdom itself is a cleansing agent (*Phaedo*, 69c).

The way of the *philosopher* is the way of gaining *wisdom*. It's not enough to know *about* things, but rather, to *know* and *understand* them—just as we are meant to *know* and *grow* in our understanding of God *directly* and not through religion. Any time a structure is put up that assures learning about Him *through* it; we can be assured it is in error. In Socrates' day, there were those doing just that. They had set up structures and built temples that initiated others on how to get to God.

> Perhaps these people who have established religious initiations are not so far from the mark, and all the time there has been **a hidden meaning beneath their claim** that he who enters the next world uninitiated and unenlightened shall lie in the mire, but he who arrives there purified and enlightened shall dwell among the gods. You know how those involved in initiations say "Many bear the emblem, but the devotees are few" (*Phaedo*, 69c).

Just like today, there are different routes of initiation to God. Perhaps the few who actually make it to Heaven and come back to tell about it convince the others that it was because of their particular initiation that they made it. But is that really the case? This is what Socrates said:

> Well, in my opinion these devotees are **simply those who have lived the philosophical life in the right way**; a company which, all through my life I have done my best in every way to join, leaving nothing undone which I could do to attain this end (*Phaedo*, 69c).

So we see, even Socrates who lived to be 70 years of age, knew many things, having been guided by the Divine Voice when he went about trying to bust people out of their limiting frameworks by challenging, questioning, and exposing their inherent weaknesses. He wasn't seeking to tear people down, but rather to bring them to philosophy to learn about reality out from behind their prison bars.

This is how it was done:

> A philosopher's soul will take the view which I have described. It will not first expect to be set free by philosophy, and then allow pleasure and pain to reduce it once more to bondage, thus condemning itself to an endless task, like Penelope, when she worked to undo her own weaving; no, this soul brings calm to the seas of desire **by following Reason and abiding always in her company, and by contemplation the true and divine and unambiguous, and drawing inspiration from it;** because such a soul believes that this is the right way to live while life endures, and that **after death it reaches a place which is kindred and similar to its own nature,** and there is rid for ever of human ills (*Phaedo*, 84a).

Socrates was absolutely aware of and sensitive to the inner spiritual workings of life—these quotes prove that—yet he had no one as his guide other than God.

Death of Socrates

Socrates, like Jesus, was brought before an open court, accused, and had the chance to revoke his teachings and change his ways. But, like Jesus, he declined.

> You know that I am not going to alter my conduct, not even if I have to die a hundred deaths (*Apology*, 30c).

Before taking the fatal cup of hemlock (a much more humane form of execution), Socrates explained to his friends how a person can be certain regarding the fate of his soul:

> These are the reasons, then, for which a man can be confident about the fate of his soul—as long as in life he has abandoned those other pleasures and adornments,

the bodily ones, as foreign to his purpose and likely to do more harm than good, and has **devoted himself to the pleasures of acquiring knowledge, and so by adorning his soul not with a borrowed beauty but with its own —with self-control, and goodness, and courage, and liberality, and truth—has settled down to await his journey to the next world** (*Phaedo*, 114e).

People can extract what they want from Socrates, and most people do; however, I have extracted what he wanted me to and good reason alone can show the truth of it. Jesus was a lover of truth; we should be lovers of truth, and the *Philosopher's Way* shows us how without the expense of our soul for structure's domination.

Socrates taught that there are laws that conduct us in life and there will be laws that control us in death. The *Philosopher's Way* is to know and follow those. Most people know about such things through religious frameworks, but if they succeed in life or in death, it is actually because of the personal application of what Socrates said: the pleasures of acquiring knowledge, self-control, goodness, courage, liberality, and truth, not just by making a confession or participating in an initiation.

We can and should pull out from structures that try to dominate and segregate us and move into the one structure that God has authorized our service in—mankind, man serving man, pleasing God. The following are some additional quotes from Socrates; some may even sound familiar.

Additional Quotes

To the council members he addressed during his trial:

> It is not a lack of arguments that has caused my condemnation, but a lack of effrontery and impudence, and the fact that I have **refused to address you in the way which would give you most pleasure**

(*Apology*, 38d).

I suggest gentlemen, that the difficulty is not so much to escape death; **the real difficulty is to escape from wickedness**, which is far more fleet afoot (*Apology*, 39b).

Socrates was both aware of, and capable of, prophesying:

I feel moved to **prophesy** to you who have given your vote against me; for I am now at that point where the **gift of prophecy** comes most readily to men: at the point of death (*Apology*, 39c).

I am no worse endowed with prophetic powers by **my master** than they are (*Phaedo*, 85b).

Nothing can harm a good man either in life or after death (*Apology*, 41d).

The really important thing is not to live, but to live well (*Crito*, 48b).

And for those who think he was talking

about extreme sports:

> It is agreed that to live well amounts to living **honorably and justly** (*Crito*, 48b).

> Philosophy is the greatest of the arts (*Phaedo*, 61a).

> True philosophers **abstain** from all bodily desires and withstand them and do not yield to them (*Phaedo*, 82c).

> The greater confidence and security by the **surer means** of a divine revelation (*Phaedo*, 85e).

Here is a wonderful report from one of his observers of what great care and skill Socrates had:

> That he should be **ready with an answer** was, I suppose, nothing unusual; but what impressed me was first, the pleasant, kindly, appreciative way in which he received the young men's thoughts, then his **quick recognition** of how

the turn of the discussion had affected us; and lastly the skill with which he **healed our wounds, rallied our scattered forces,** and **encouraged us** to join him in pursuing the inquiry.

Leaving nothing undone to attain during life some measure of goodness and wisdom; for the **prize is glorious** and the hope great (*Phaedo,* 114c).

As for my long and elaborate explanation that when I have drunk the poison I shall remain with you no longer, but depart to a **world of happiness that belongs to the blessed,** my words seem to be wasted on him though I console both you and myself (*Phaedo,* 114d).

I would like to share a final word then a poem. Just as I was driving home from the airport coming back from Athens the Father blessed me with this final revelation. When Jesse Duplantis met Paul in Heaven, he said that Paul referred to the gospel as "his gospel." Jesse took note of that. Now, the Father wanted me to take note of it. The gospel according to Paul is not **the** gospel of Jesus Christ but what Paul did with the gospel. We have no need to base anything exclusively on what Paul or Peter did, only on what Jesus said.

Next time denominations want to argue over points of doctrine, they need to restrict their reasoning only to what Jesus said. This was a major revelation to my soul, and I put it next to the Book of Mormon and what Jesus said there. By combining the gospels with Third Nephi, we have the base gospel. Everything else are points of reference only. I want to thank our Father for this broader view and for helping my understanding of it. I pray that it may be a blessing to others as well, as we all seek Your glory, God, and the unifying of Your children, Father.

I thank our Savior for introducing me to Socrates, and I thank Socrates for his hospitality. It has not been easy for any of them to go so far back in time to assist my

understanding of how things were back
then, so I give them all the praise!

Sunset in Olympia - Final Night

Master of your Soul

The master of your soul is God

Serve God

God does not dwell in structures

Structures do not contain God

We are made in His image

He has eyes to see

Ears to hear

A heart to feel

He is neither deaf, dumb, or blind

If we do well

He will accept us

If we are compatible

We will join Him

If we have abilities

He will use them

Use Reason

Gain Wisdom

Journey 20 - New Jerusalem Fulfilled

Albany, New York

To my closest friends, I write a prelude to the work that will yet go forth. You will marvel at the graciousness of God to condescend and send help from above, to help our unbelief. "God, help my unbelief," they all cried out. Well, now your cry for help has been answered! My friends, you who know me well know that I always petition God and always seek His love, and whenever He chooses to give it, I always rejoice in it. For our God is a God of Love, the most wonderful of emotions that a person can have, and when He gives it forth, it is always pure and flows into the inner most part of our being.

There is no greater love felt than when a person feels they belong to God!

God has condescended to reward us with knowledge of where we are and, in particular, where we are with the Book of Mormon. Because the book contains the "Vision of All" as foretold by Isaiah, we know it tells all, including where we are. And where are we? That is something the religionists of our day do not know, and yet they joyfully go on their way spreading false truths and misleading information.

It is a crime to say something is yet to be fulfilled when all of Heaven knows it has *already been fulfilled*. I am referring to the *New Jerusalem* to be built on the *Promised Land*. However, if you know not *where* the promised lands are, then you are foolish for what you are teaching.

Praise God for hearing my prayer, and the prayers of *millions* for *decades* and sending His chosen servant, Moroni (a translated, not resurrected being) to give me understanding. Like other translated beings on assignment, Moroni is *very* engaged and *anxious* to do the work he has been called to do. Translated beings petition God all the time for His permission to solicit workers in a just cause, but God will not grant their every request, just as He will not grant our every desire. But when He does, we surely all rejoice, just as we rejoiced after God granted Moroni permission to recruit me in this cause.

Part of God's work is based upon the labors done by this man and Joseph Smith. I am now a part of that same work, and this part was long ago foretold and is recorded in Scripture for those who want to know. There is no mistaking it, this was all *foreknown* and *foretold*.

Book of Mormon Lands

The lands of the Book of Mormon must be known in order to understand how the prophecies in it and about it are being fulfilled. The existing mindset among ALL groups of Book of Mormon believers is that they occurred in Mesoamerica. To God and His children that lived it, **THAT IS RIDICULOUS**.

How misled can people be about the things of God? How deceived can they be regarding His Spirit? Just look at all the people who believe "they know" it all occurred down in Mexico, Panama and South America. Many are the stories being told of alleged spiritual manifestations in support of those claims, and who do we think is filling their minds with that information? **IT IS NOT GOD, AND CURSED BE THEY WHO PERVERT THE WAYS OF GOD!** For if we are only seeking to do our will and not His, we will be hindering His plan to bring true understanding and unity.

187

I testify that the angel Moroni did come to me and he did invite me to his homeland and he did show me many things essential to receiving a true witness of these things. At the same time, I did visit many of the Mormon Church history sites associated with Joseph Smith, and I will share *some* of those as I go along. All these things have already been known, but now I will document them with pictures, dates, etc. We are fulfilling prophecy and will continue to help others fulfill prophecy also. How we do that is up to us, but so far we are laying a strong foundation.

So let me take you from the east to the west, just as Moroni took me. I was first told when to fly and where to go. The date was November 12, and I was only given about a week's notice. I was also told that of all trips I have taken, this trip would be the most complex to understand, and I was commanded to prepare myself well before going (by complex, he meant many different but related topics).

So, I labored diligently on the different areas of focus the week prior to going and did not rest at night, the power of anticipation being nearly overwhelming. Neither could my wife sleep; our days were full of anticipation. Nevertheless, I did as I was commanded, and these are the different areas I was commanded to focus on:

1. Early Colonial History

2. Early American Indian History

3. Early LDS Church History

4. Book of Mormon Geography

Like I said, many of these things I had already learned, but now I was going to have them documented and I testify that in none of these things did I learn them from anyone else except from God and His servants, and He allowed me to connect the dots. If there are others who understand one or more areas as I do, then they may know God confirms these truths.

Albany

I was commanded to fly into Albany, and I spent two nights and one day there. As always, I did not know where I would be going, so I usually am unable to make hotel reservations beforehand, but in all things Moroni knew exactly where I should go and where I should stay, and so I did follow his lead.

One of the things I was also told to do was to bring a copy of the *Original Book of Mormon* and place it within the picture of key sites. I will not enclose those pictures here, but I did as I was commanded and I have pictures of the book at the place of the *Three Witnesses*, the *Hill Cumorah Monument*, and the *State Capital Building* where I was now going.

Without a map, Moroni led me to my hotel, then to parks, plaques, museums, visitor centers, etc., in order to obtain all the necessary information to document what prophecies are fulfilled here. I testify that under the direction of Almighty God I did do as I was commanded and that the following facts are true:

1. **Albany is the eastern corridor to ancient Book of Mormon lands**.

2. **Albany is the *birth place* of the *New Jerusalem* with Benjamin Franklin's *Albany Plan of Union,* which grew into our government of the United States.**

3. **Albany is still the center place and the place where the *New Jerusalem* above will come**.

As all of Heaven looks down, this is what they see in confirmation of the center place of the *New Jerusalem* —**Empire Plaza**, inspired and uniquely designed to stand out from ALL other cities on earth, and it does. Just imagine my surprise when I saw the following structures:

Empire State Plaza

In all things done by God or man, they start small then grow large. At what point in that growing process does God say the prophecy is fulfilled? All Book of Mormon believing groups are still waiting for this part regarding the *New Jerusalem* to be fulfilled and yet it has ALREADY been fulfilled by the government of the United States.

Bleecker Park

I almost forgot, this is a park in Albany that Joseph told me he had been to. It is southwest of the Empire Plaza, right across the street from the Cathedral of Immaculate Conception.

Iroquois Nation

The second part of this prophecy has to do with the Native Americans in that area. They were to found a New Jerusalem with the white Gentiles, but

God needed to unify them first. As God started the *Reformation* among the Gentiles with *Martin Luther, John Calvin, Huldrych Zwingli,* and others, He brought unity and peace among the warring Indian tribes on Book of Mormon lands by the *Great Peacemaker (Deganawida).*

The *Great Peacemaker* was a prophet sent by God to unify the tribes on the *Promised Land.* I went to *Lake Onondaga,* where the culmination of his efforts did unite the tribes. All tribes agreed to bury their weapons beneath the *Tree of Peace Forever.*

THE IROQUOIS CONFEDERACY

The northeast shore of Onondaga Lake has traditionally been recognized as the site of the founding of the Iroquois Confederacy in the late 16th century. Hiawatha, revered by the Iroquois as "the Peacemaker," was responsible for bringing together the Five Nations in a political and military league.

The Confederation allowed the Iroquois to develop the most sophisticated political system in North America by the time European colonization began. The military power of the Iroquois expanded as well. At its peak in the late 17th century, the Confederacy was able to assert itself over native peoples from New England to the Mississippi and from the St. Lawrence Valley to Virginia. The Iroquois remained a significant power in North America until their defeat in the American Revolution. The strength of the Confederacy forged by Hiawatha is still evident. Despite military defeat and the loss of their lands, the Iroquois nations continue to hold council in Onondaga County as they have for nearly 400 years.

As I traveled there, I was blessed to see in Spirit how this great prophet came across *Lake Ontario* and was a descendant of the people of Hagoth. He went from village to village by the power of God unifying the warring tribes (later a sixth tribe was added), and as a whole, they became known as the *Six Nations*, *Iroquois Confederacy of Nations*, or *Haudenosaunee Confederacy*.

Yes, the Great Peacemaker *did* prepare the way, and the Iroquois did establish a working relationship with the Gentiles when they arrived; their treaties still exist (e.g., *Treaty of Canandaigua*). They are a sovereign nation separate from the United States government, and we co-exist with them upon ancient Book of Mormon lands. **Without them, the Colonists would have never defeated the British and gained their independence as long ago foretold**.

Geography

One of the biggest problems believers in the Book of Mormon have is agreeing where the lands are. Every church who uses the Book of Mormon believes the events occurred in Mesoamerica. Yet as I have testified before and will here testify again, they are all wrong and are being led by deceiving spirits because they do

197

not follow the teachings in the Book of Mormon. Moroni was allowed by God to show me two things—where the Book of Mormon began, and where it ended. In-between those two points I did visit historical sites like *Harmony, PA*, where Emma lived and where the Book of Mormon was partly transmitted.

From *Harmony* I went to *Lake Seneca*, and here Moroni showed me where he fled at the end of his life. He stayed locally after the final Nephite battle and became what he described was a type of mayor in present-day *Geneva*. He was revered by the locals and protected until one day his past enemies discovered his location (keep in mind, they did not have cell phones, cameras, or any way to take pictures or communicate over long distances then). He had previously stowed away a canoe at the north edge of the lake and escaped by canoe to the lake's south edge and then fled into a gorge in *Watkins Glen* where he narrowly escaped. There within the gorge he was taken-up, *never tasting death*.

Watkins Glen is now a state park and a popular tourist attraction because of its many beautiful waterfalls. Here are a few pictures of it.

This is looking from, I believe, the court house; the gorge is between the hill straight ahead and the other hill on the left.

This is what the main entrance looks like, with a tunnel on the right and the exiting waterfall on the left.

This is looking at the same entrance further down the river that has exited the gorge. This is what Moroni saw as he approached the gorge and followed the river up into it.

This is the spot in which he was standing when he was taken up.

A typical view of the gorge. Next I will show some views of Seneca Lake.

This is the south side of the lake. It is now a marina.

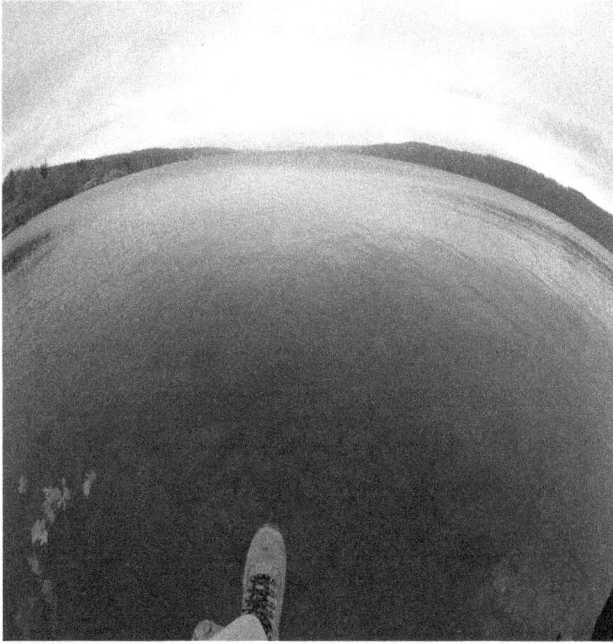

My view of the lake and the clear water, looking northward.

This would have been Moroni's view as he approached the south end of the lake, with a view of the hill on the right and the gorge immediately behind. This was a well-planned, well–thought out escape route.

After Moroni was taken up, he showed me his immediate view from above, as several of his adversaries were going along the top of the gorge trying to find a way in. (Moroni had a ladder to get up and in the gorge that he then pulled up behind him.) I learned much about his enemies. They wanted nothing less than **absolute extinction** of that white race and took great pride in bringing it about!!

From there I went to the Whitmer home where the remainder of the Book of Mormon was translated and where the Three Witnesses saw the record for themselves. I testify that this event did indeed take place there, and the Glory can still be felt as well, even though the original trees and forest are clearly gone. Many other things happened here as well as in Harmony that I could comment on, but I must save for another time.

From there I drove on to Cumorah and for the first time I got to see the hill and related sites. At this juncture in the writing of this synopsis, I am told to pause, and so I retire promptly. Then, at 2:00 in the morning I am awakened from my sleep due to lots of commotion and exchanges and I am told to remember the names of two men. However, I am very tired and go back to sleep. Then, all through the rest of the night I hear the name Thomas Paine called out, OVER and OVER again, until I awake. This name I would not forget, for how could I, it was repeated so many times during my sleep that I finally awoke to see what I could learn about this man that had to be included and honored for the part he played in the founding of the *New Jerusalem*.

So I pause here to share what I have learned, and I do marvel that he is not better known for the contributions that he made for the cause. As so many times before, I testify that I did not know any of these things about this man, and I am sure there is so much more to be known about him, but these are the truths Moroni wants to be made known.

Thomas Paine

Born in 1737 in England, he came to America in 1774 at the behest of Benjamin Franklin. I found an interesting quote that he gave:

> I saw, or at least I thought **I saw, a vast scene opening** itself to the world in the affairs of America, and it appeared to me that unless the Americans changed the plan they were pursuing with respect to the government of England and declared themselves independent, they would shut out the prospect that was then offering itself to mankind through their means (*The*

Age of Reason, 1793, Part I).

In any case, it appears that Paine had a view others did not, and it was he who could appreciate what this new country had to offer and the terrible proposition if the British crown ruled. Others who had lived in the new country for years no doubt could not see the forest for the trees. However, Paine could and did. It was Paine who widely published the words: "Declare Independence" in his pamphlet *Common Sense* (January 10, 1776).

That pamphlet (he authored it anonymously) sold more than 600,000 copies to a population of 3,000,000, twenty percent of whom were slaves and fifty percent indentured servants. It is a good read and available at most bookstores as well as online. He received no remuneration for it. Based upon this and his other writings, it is now believed that Paine was the author of our *Declaration of Independence*. However, Thomas Jefferson received the credit and presented it. So Paine catapulted the independence movement by his booklet and then authored in part or full its founding document.

During the *Revolutionary War*, when Washington was being beaten, he received two kinds of help: food support from the Iroquois and moral support from the words of Thomas Paine in *The American Crisis*. Here is one such quote:

> **These are the times that try men's souls**. The summer soldier and the sunshine patriot will, in this crisis, shrink from the service of his country; but he that stands it NOW deserves the love and thanks of man and woman. Tyranny, like hell, is not easily conquered; yet we have this consolation with us, that the harder the conflict, the more glorious the triumph. What we obtain too cheap, we esteem too lightly: 'tis dearness only that gives everything its value. Heaven knows how to put a proper price upon its goods; and it would be strange indeed if so celestial an

article as FREEDOM should not be highly rated.

Those are the very words that helped to win the war, and it is said that they were the words on the *lips of every soldier as they battled*.

There is much more to be attributed to this man, but all in all, he has purposely been left out of history for his lack of religious favoritism. He was also instrumental in starting the French Revolution by the same means that he helped the American Revolution. To verify the good Paine did we have this *Congressional Resolution* dated August 26, 1785:

> *Resolved*, That the early, unsolicited and continued labors of Mr. Thomas Paine, in explaining and enforcing the principles of the late Revolution, by the ingenious and timely publications upon the nature of liberty and civil government, have been well received by the citizens of these States, and merit

the approbation of Congress; and the benefits produced thereby, Mr. Paine is entitled to a liberal gratification from the United States.

Paine did receive sums of money and land in appreciation. So, too, did Congress acknowledge the help the Iroquois provided in the war. These are interesting parallels that deserve our attention, and I will try to give them the attention they deserve. Paine encouraged the purchase of Louisiana and first coined the name *United States of America (thomaspaine.org)*. I found this quote by John Adams:

History is to ascribe the American Revolution to Thomas Paine (John H. Hazelton, *The Declaration of Independence*, 1906).

Or this regarding the French:

In the spring of 1790, Paine visited Paris. He found the French people still rejoicing over the fall of the

Bastille. Lafayette assured him that its overthrow was due entirely to the transfer of American principles to France, and presented him with the key to the old fortress. On the first of May, Paine returned to London and sent the key to General Washington. It now rests in Washington's old home at Mount Vernon (*THEOSOPHY*, vol. 27, no. 2, December 1938).

Lastly, I found this quote by Paine:

My country is the world, and my religion is to do good (Rights of Man).

Though ascribed as being an atheist, I think there is more to his story than meets the eye, but for his place in establishing the *New Jerusalem*, I believe it has been well established that he was its leading cause—*and that by God*. Praise be to God for sending this man at the right moment, who chose by the inspiration of God the right words to use in his pamphlets—*even the name of our country*. I look forward to learning more about him. For now, I return to the journey.

First Vision

Some of you know from my recent correspondence that God showed me and taught me to appreciate the "First Vision" of Joseph Smith. In a nutshell, God our Father has never come down to man before aside from our father Adam, which was in a different time and dimension. The only reason that our Father did come down was to jump-start **His own work** known in the Book of Mormon as the "Work of the Father." In the *Holy Bible* it is called "A Marvelous Work and A Wonder." In any case, I was shown the place and Joseph's view when he left it before I went there. Having never been to New York or these church sites, it was all new to me.

I did a quick tour through the "Sacred Grove," but other than the location where the Eight Witnesses had a view of the ancient record, our Father's glory was not there. I continued to walk around looking

215

for His glory. One thing Joseph had showed me was that it was south of his farm, and so I proceeded to walk south a great distance from the Sacred Grove.

Finally, off in the distance above the tree lines I saw the Glory of our Father and so I went closer. There, beyond the edge of their property, was a plowed field and at the edge of that field tall trees, and it was in that vicinity that the glorious appearing of God the Father and Jesus Christ originally took place. Here is a picture of that view:

I was shown the young boy Joseph whom I describe as having the mentality of a 12-year-old, and I followed him all the way home, including his view, how he felt, etc. All these things are known in Spirit. I then toured the two homes that the family lived in. I also went to the farm of Martin Harris and there, too, did I confirm what Joseph showed me when he went to work there. Everything was located just as he had previously shown me.

There are two prominent things:

1. The belief and support of Martin Harris.

2. The belief and support of the Whitmer family.

Only those who walk by faith alone can know how it feels to finally have confirmations and support. Those are HUGE emotional moments.

Cumorah

The hill itself is not that tall but then again I am used to climbing mountains. All pictures I have ever seen of it made it look much larger. I was also surprised by the width of the hill along the top; it was quite narrow. In fact, that monument covers the whole width of it.

This indeed was the highest view of all other hills and the main point of view in war time as well. The left or west and north of this view would be toward the battle field, with the domestic preparations where women and children remained to the east behind it. As you look north, you see small rolling hills (and I mean barley rolling small) and some scattered drumlin hills like what Cumorah is on.

Just as I was shown regarding the account of Zelph, this outer lying area for miles and miles was relatively flat and brown, just bare dirt, that went for miles back then. Now, it is of course green everywhere and trees plenty. I dare say ANYONE could stand on that hill and imagine the final Nephite battle taking place there and not in Mesoamerica. I was also shown the location of the record and Joseph's view when he first saw the plates. Moroni also blessed me with his view, and I look forward to describing that as well. It is amazing, ancient history that IS REAL! Now here we are today, what are we going to do?

I will say this though, at the Visitor's Center and in SLC, I am very appreciative of all that the LDS church has done to promote the Book of Mormon, and I think it is marvelous that there is a pageant there on the hill and everything else, for this record deserves every bit of celebration as that **AND A WHOLE LOT MORE.**

I believe we could recommend the Cumorah Visitor's Center to Christians without them getting offended by "the only true church" stuff. Here is a picture from inside:

Joseph Smith's First Vision

"I saw a pillar of light exactly over my head, above the brightness of the sun, which descended gradually until it fell upon me. . . . When the light rested upon me I saw two personages, whose brightness and glory defy all description, standing above me in the air. One of them spake unto me, calling me by name and said, pointing to the other— 'This is my beloved Son. Hear him!'"

Joseph Smith—History 1:16–17

We must respect the First Vision!

There were awesome displays on The Book everywhere, and only one on the "restoration."

This is a picture of the Smith property with the road down the middle and a curvy line for the creek. The dark area on the left is the "Sacred Grove" with the true Sacred Grove being south of their property line altogether and not so far to the left.

Now on to the last part of the journey. I was in a great hurry to get to Kirtland then to fly out. However, in my rush:

I encountered a snow storm west of Buffalo:

And nearly crashed the car as so many others had. I was taking pictures of all the spinouts and collisions, but there were so many I gave up. Then, after my own spinout across all three lanes back and forth four times, I somehow escaped without hitting anything or going off the road. Praise God for all those prayers, for they were called in at that moment.

Moroni told me to stop in Erie, which is barely across the Pennsylvania border. As I approached, I decided not to as I was ahead of all the traffic and making great progress on my way to Kirtland before the Kirtland Temple Visitor's Center closed. However, as I approached the exit and said those words, Moroni became angry with me and commanded me to get off. I then said to Moroni, "What is here?" at which he replied, "This is where Lehi's ship landed." Wow!!!!!!! Now that was worth not missing, so I did as I was commanded and made my way to the points he directed.

Here is a picture of the bay they sailed into:

I know it is not much, but Moroni said this image will be memorable. You see the water out there, well beyond that is a marina and beyond that, Lake Erie.

Here is a nice sign for Erie:

Well, I am sure you can imagine my extreme joy at that information and when the history of the whole thing began to unfold unto me. Unfortunately, I was tapped out from all the driving in the snow and nearly killing myself so I promised I would pursue the greater understanding at another time. On the peninsula of that bay, which really is quite large, is a state park, a wonderful place. We can easily trace the journeys of Nephi and his family who escaped into the wilderness and we can trace all over unto Cumorah and the place where Moroni was removed.

I look forward to giving the geography a fresh new look, but overall, my understanding was very close. I thank Moroni and the Father for giving us this much information for **many** people have prayed asking about it. Imagine how dumb everyone else looks purporting Mesoamerican lands—it is ridiculous and hurtful. We know what voice they are hearing, and it is not God.

I did make it to Kirtland with a great deal of effort, but of course everything had been closed for hours. Still I did want to see the spot and look for what glory was there. This was another momentous occasion. Why? Because just imagine, you have a group of supporters but no church building! What is the first thing all new churches do today? They start building. So did Joseph's people, but it was a "temple" not a church; they never built churches back then.

The glory revealed there, the Father told me, was nothing more than what can and does occur whenever you have a group of sincere believers. The cause originates with their sincerity not with the building. The key here is that He said it happens all the time—meaning in all denominations, etc. I thought of Henry Gruver who was preaching in a church right there in Arizona and was taken up into Heaven before all of them and landed on streets paved with gold and was allowed to approach the throne of God.

I then looked across the road from the

temple and there was a Community of Christ chapel, and to the right of it Sydney Rigdon's home. Then I remembered how he showed me he would go there every day. That was his intimate spot. Then he said to me as I contemplated his lot:

> Every man has a right to share his view of the gospel of Jesus Christ, and that is how I justify my lot.

We all have a right to tell our view, and nobody's view is right or wrong; it is just their current view. There is only one regret I have of this whole trip and that is that I did not go to the cemetery that was next door to the temple. There was GREAT SADNESS associated with it and I know that Joseph and Emma's twins are buried there plus other family members. There was great sadness for them in Harmony because of the loss of their firstborn child, and sadly enough, they were revisited with the loss of twins in Kirtland.

Even now as I am writing I am sad for them and mad that I did not make the effort to find their sites and pay my respects. I did take a picture from a distance, but I know that Emma wanted me to do more than that. Well, that is all I am allowed to share for now and should suffice to settle all disputes regarding the Book of Mormon and to clarify some LDS church history and doctrine.

Journey 21 - Western New York

I returned to western New York the following year and was privileged to meet Moroni again (and others) and travel throughout that area and learn about what rich Book of Mormon history there remains untapped. If you view Joseph Smith's early travels and developments, it will be seen that with every non-Book of Mormon doctrine that he taught and embraced he was being removed from Holy Book of Mormon lands and taken deeper into Lamanite lands until ultimately he was buried in an ancient Lamanite burial mound, which remains to this day the largest symbol of with whom he aligned himself.

Not only that, but he died on the anniversary of the implementation of the so-called "Melchizedek Priesthood" (see Wilford C. Wood, *Joseph Smith Begins His Work*).

After landing in Rochester with no plans of where to go or stay (besides a car rental) Moroni instructed me to the

233

Genesee River closest to the *Rochester Airport* and there I found a park that rented boats. He said to rent a canoe and I want you to experience what we did when we traveled down the river in our canoes. So I did as he instructed and mounted a video camera to the canoe (and later the dash of the car) and filmed all my travels.

It was a long paddle to reach the downtown area where there are waterfalls; I could not travel by boat farther. The time it took to paddle there and back gave me space to settle my nerves, expend excess energy, talk with Moroni, and contemplate what lay ahead. The following morning we headed south out of *Rochester,* and Moroni commanded me to follow, observe, and record the Genesee River (this is important because some Book of Mormon geography enthusiasts claim it was the "River Sidon").

There were many Indian historical markers along the way and plenty of farm land. Eventually we arrived at the "Grand

Canyon of the East" which is *Letchworth State Park*. At this location, it was clear that this could not be nor ever was the ancient *River Sidon* (and no one would consider it if they had truly traveled the length of it). You could not walk down to the water let alone baptize in it or fight with the enemy "along its banks." This was the "Sea East" which was the eastern border for most of Book of Mormon lands (and subsequent Indian tribes).

We went from the east side of the river, and once we could cross back to the west side, we did so.

It is an exceptionally unique and beautiful park. We stopped at one of the high points and looked back toward Rochester from where we had come, and I was greeted by Mormon. Mormon then described his call to keep the records. When he was young, he was instructed to go to a certain place in Rochester to learn about the "Hall of Records." I saw in spirit this time in his life and his travels, where he stopped and where he went. Moroni then said we would visit the ancient Hall of Records tomorrow.

It was now dark, so I slept in the car. Early the next morning I made my way into the area of Rochester along the river and ended up at the highest spot where

Ether hid and recorded the final days of the Jaredite nation. I saw how he lived, that he had both a laying hen and a goat that he kept tied up and which provide him with basic sustenance as well as edible plants and such. I was shown the final days of the prophet Ether and observed his routine; he could literally see the battle going on down below across the river and remained hidden all the days of his life (as did Moroni, explained further down).

The fighting armies were exhausted EVERY night, and so he could go down, cross the river, and walk among the dead and see what had taken place. He did this day after day until, as he said, they were all dead. Thus, from this knowledge I learned that the Jaredite final battle happened on the west side of the Genesee River, while the Nephite final battle happened as it says near the Hill Cumorah. Early settlers of Rochester did in fact report that they could hardly put a spade in the earth and not uncover bones and many that were giant in size. This whole scene was much to take in; but that's how it was.

Then Moroni wanted to show me a gravestone (for we were in a cemetery). He said this was the first person buried on this special hill because it was wisdom in God that it and the Hall of Records be protected and by becoming a cemetery it would! [Update: Moroni has since informed me that those records have been "eternalized" which means God took them much like He saved Moroni by translation.]

"This child aged 4 Y, 2 M died Oct. 3, 1832, at 2:30 p.m.—the precise time when this cemetery was consecrated & his was the first body buried in it after its consecration." As can be seen, the inscription was on the side of the tombstone and not easily seen, but Moroni knew its history, significance, and where it was located (and I suspect he played a part in it). From here Moroni took me down to where he lived and stayed, like Ether, for many years and his routine of going down to the river for water and such. From the moment I entered the cemetery to the minute I left, I could see that it was saturated with the glory of God, which also goes undetected because of it being a cemetery and presumably holy which is disguising the underlying holiness that traces back to Moroni, to Mormon, and ultimately to Ether.

When a person enters the cemetery, this is what they see:

Continuing past the chapel, a person sees this:

The next picture represents the *Hall of Records*:

After this we went next door to the university, and Moroni wanted me to see something: their "Faith Center" where people of different faiths meet; *one building is used by them all.*

241

He said during Book of Mormon times they did "church" differently. They had one place for worship, which was usually around the camp fire, and anyone could join in and everyone participated in their singing and dancing to God. There was a place where people studied the law, and "church" was not in a building but was just neighbors looking out for each other and meeting in a very intimate setting (their homes) and that was restricted to the faithful only.

After showing me other sites and taking many pictures and video, we began to travel the roads of western New York (filming as we went) and tracing to the head of every water way that flowed into Lake Ontario, one of which is Oak Orchard Harbor:

He said this river, even in his time, was a coveted spot during the Salmon runs. It was also a rite of passage for many young men to venture out on their own, find the river, trace it down to the lake where much trading would take place and then return with food, tools, trinkets and whatever else they could obtain. Though Moroni did not say where the traders came from (and I did not think to ask), I had the sense that some traders came by canoe.

Also at this location was a sign about the War of 1812:

Moroni pointed out the significance of
it, saying that it fulfilled Book of Mormon
prophecy that the "mother countries
would come to battle against the colonist
upon the land and sea," both of which

were fulfilled right there in western New York, Lake Ontario, and Lake Erie.

Attica

What I am going to share next requires some background and was one of the darkest times of my experience touring ancient Book of Mormon lands. Though I had gone across ancient battle fields, those horrific scenes were shielded from my view (which I gave thanks for), but not this. In fact, even before I left on this trip, I was being warned and attacked by evil forces there in western New York. At the time I did not understand the *where* or the *why*, but I was shown that I would come face-to-face with extreme wickedness in spirit, and I was shown that it would be raining when I came.

Thus far on my trip I had not experience any rain, which I was grateful for, for I did not want to come face-to-face with whatever this evil was, and I was shown in vision it would happen on a dark and dreary, rainy day. After our travels the rest of that day, Moroni left me to myself, and I continued into the night and then there came before me a clear vision of what I could only describe as a "prison" of extremely dark and trapped souls. (regardless of what a person's view is on where the departed dead are, I clearly saw trapped souls who were being tormented in some sort of hell on earth).

And just as I was shown in vision before I left that it would be raining when I arrived at the location, it had begun to rain. I finally ended at my destination without a clue where I was or what it was, for it was very dark and raining, and I was just as tired. I pulled the car off the road and slept what I could through the rest of the night. When I awoke, I was shocked to see that I had mysteriously driven to and had parked across from a literal prison: *Attica Correctional Facility.*

I could not believe my eyes, let alone the extreme evil that permeated the area in spirit. Moroni revealed to me that this prison was actually built over an ancient Lamanite prison and is where they imprisoned and tortured Nephites in the most horrific way as detailed in the Book of Mormon. He also said that proof of the ancient prison could be found within the prison and he assured me that a simple radar ground scan would prove it.

Attica Correctional Facility from above:

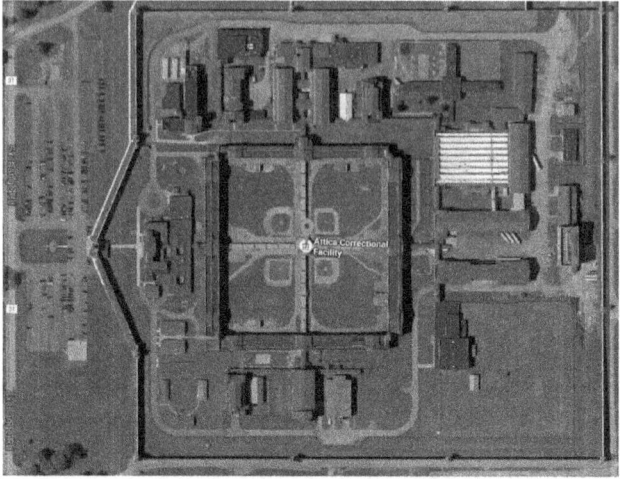

I was and still am disturbed by what I saw and believe that a living human can and must take authority over the evil that exists there and set those trapped souls free. Because I am not experienced in something of that scale, I was not able to do anything at the time, but I believe it is my duty to do something about it, and so I shall.

The next day Moroni showed me where the ancient city of Zarahemla was and the true River Sidon. He said there are archaeological remains all over the place and home owners almost never report what they find due to existing laws. He showed me the hills (or mountains) of wilderness not far from Zarahemla where the wicked Lamanites lived and who would come into the Nephite lands and plunder their belongings.

We drove up into some of the homes currently in such areas, and he brought me to one house in particular and explained that this home owner built a pond in his back yard and discovered unusual gold artifacts; he told no one. He showed me in vision the episode and I could not believe it. It did not look as if anyone was home so I drove to their driveway and could see into the back yard (which was large and woodsy), and sure enough there was a pond. I took note of the address and plan on contacting the owner when the time is right.

We went through the many hills surrounding Zarahemla, and I understood why it was easy to get lost traveling to and from the city of Nephi. We only went along the edge of the Land of Nephi where there is an Indian reservation, and he showed my an ancient burial mound that is being protected by the tribe. Said Moroni, "When the time is right, many archaeological discoveries will be found in that mound that will support the Book of Mormon."

We continued filming the streets back and forth across the rest of western New York, and I should say at this time that I was commanded to fast during the trip and I slept very little in the car each night. As we were finishing the survey of the land, I ended up as far west as you can go, which brought me to where the Niagara River and Gorge flow into Lake Ontario; at that location is Fort Niagara. When we drove into the parking lot of the fort, there was no one around, and the sun was about to set. I had been fasting many days and had endured a roller-coaster of emotions and was physically, mentally, and spiritually exhausted.

Unbeknownst to me, everything in my daily travels had been planned so that I would arrive at that location on that day and that time. When I got out of the car, Moroni left me, and to my great surprise,

I was met by Jesus. He came from above and said, "I am going to show you what happened when I appeared to the Nephites after my resurrection." With that, I was taken back in time to see what the locals saw. Up above, over Lake Ontario, is where Our Lord literally split the sky and was accompanied by a host of angels and the cloud of witnesses and was seen in glory.

I had been to the Garden Tomb in Jerusalem and saw where Our Lord had came forth from the grave and where His glory and presence can still be felt, but this was magnified a hundred times more because He came in glory and purposely flexed or demonstrated His power, and that coupled with the fact that it happened over the lake where no one and nothing can pollute its spiritual energy residue, it remains strong. That area and the falls is associated with love but like with the cemetery, the falls are hiding or masking the underlying powerful feeling of love; that is the strong imprint of Our Lord's love.

There is a large grassy area that slowly descends to the water, and I stood all alone basking in the residue of Our Lord's love, spirit, and glory.

My fasting led to this marvelous event, and I was refreshed and filled with God's love. I then sat down and continued to bask when all of the sudden I heard a loud cracking sound, and the entire earth shook for a period of time. I stood to my feet and turned around toward the sound, for it greatly startled me. Now it was dark and I was left to myself, so again I slept in the car on the side of the road determined to investigate where that noise had come from (at this point I did not realize I was by the falls).

I would like to clarify that the encounter I saw of Our Lord descending is not what is recorded in the Book of Mormon. The righteous in *Bountiful* whom Our Lord visited is the account that we have, not this first one on the edge of Lake Ontario (*Jaredite Land Northward*). The area south and slightly east of Fort Niagara is currently undeveloped but in Book of Mormon times heavily populated and I suspect full of archaeological ruins (but Moroni did not disclose that there were any).

In the morning, I began to drive along the Niagara River and document its size and terrain. All of that land slowly rises from Lake Ontario until you reach what is described now as the "escarpment." This is where the land abruptly goes up many feet as if the ground just "split in half." And in fact, it was at that moment that I learned what the huge "cracking" sound was that I had heard the night before and the cause of the shaking of the ground.

That was a tremendous display of Our Lord's power to all who were with Him:

a. He floated in the sky over Lake Ontario.

b. He stretched forth His hands to purposely demonstrate His power.

c. He literally split the rocks "both above and below the earth" as prophesied in the Book of Mormon.

d. It (and particularly the resultant waterfalls) were to ever remain a witness of Our Lord's coming.

Needless to say, my tour of the falls was joyful, and I had a big smile on my face the entire time, for what I knew, the public did not know, and yet we both marveled at and enjoyed those falls. I wanted to get some pictures of how the land was literally "split" and "lifted up," so I crossed into Canada and proceeded to travel in reverse of what I had just done and drove back toward Lake Ontario, albeit on the other side of the Niagara River.

I got as far as I could, a corner where the river and lake met where a lovely golf course sits, and I got out of the car, walked up to the water, and looked out and took pictures. With no warning whatsoever, but still in the strong presence of the Spirit of Our Lord, I saw in vision the ship that Lehi's family had sailed to the New World in. It was almost as if I were in a helicopter flying right to it. Then I was given the view of the person most strongly affected by the Liahona telling them to "turn here," Nephi's wife!

From her view I experienced that fateful moment for which they had been waiting a long time. Lake Ontario is large, almost like an ocean for you cannot see where it ends. They had been traveling along its coast passing by one harbor after another always wondering "is this it?" But the answer for days was always, "No." But this time the answer came back "Yes," so there was great elation. I saw that Nephi's family had the front of the ship and his ugly brothers the back.

It was a large ship, and I saw chickens on the deck in cages and garments on clothes lines, a kitchen area with knife and cutting board and children playing around. Everyone was per-occupied, sleeping, or exhausted except for Nephi's wife. She spotted the entrance and kept her focus after it was clear the time had come to turn. I shall never forget the elation on her face and the excitement that burst forth from her lips. That corner, the VERY CORNER where I was standing, is what her eyes focused upon when she experienced those emotions, and so they are all tied together.

What I learned of Nephi's wife is she was a proud woman (in the right way), a Hebrew, who had high expectations of "ownership" for their "promised" lands. She was beautiful, clean, tidy, educated, proper (if that makes sense) with a strong faith in their destiny and the promises of God; she owned it. They sailed up that river before there were any falls. After the coming of Jesus, that way for boats became blocked making Book of Mormon lands even more "hidden" and protected as was prophesied it would be until the Gentiles were led there by God.

After I toured the coastline along Lake Erie, the trip was coming to a close and the final place Moroni wanted me to see was where ancient River Sidon emptied into the ancient Sea West or Lake Erie. At that precise point, he brought me to a plaque on which was an engraving of a "wampum belt" given to President George Washington in a formal treaty between the Iroquois Nation and the Colonists, as was prophesied in the Book of Mormon. They would together build a New Jerusalem on ancient Book of Mormon lands:

Close up:

With that, Moroni let me go into a nearby restaurant and eat. Then I slept in the car and in the morning we ventured back east, but the time for crisscrossing the hills and valleys and videotaping the land had come to an end. Now he wanted me to see how he and others traveled from east to west and vice versa. He explained that back then a person *could* go over the many hills and valleys to get from one side to the other, but those were heavily wooded areas and difficult to traverse. They could also go north to the "superhighway," which was open, flat, and easy to travel. While it was further away, he said, overall travel times were usually less.

He then showed me a time in his life when he traversed the superhighway. I saw and felt the environment, the sun, and how God's Spirit did light upon him as he traveled; I am quite familiar with such hikes. It was clear overhead, unlike most areas in Book of Mormon lands in the Land Southward that were full of mountains / hills (and their shadows) and tall trees (and their shadows). Then I saw how this superhighway came to be. Their lands were divided north to south by a large inland sea (or lake) that was not terribly deep and was more of a giant swamp (ancient Lake Tonawanda) that you could neither walk through nor boat on.

As it receded, it left a long, flat, dried-mud plain that was ideal for traveling, and it provided an expansive view that could greatly expand one's mind as they traversed it. We then traveled to the east side of the Genesee River because he wanted me to see where he was and how the final Nephite battle took place. He said the enemy came from two sides, on the north by boat and the west by foot.

He showed me where his last camp was before his people became overrun. His campsite was built into the side of a small hill (not the top so as to be seen by the enemy) and was composed of a cave with a small fire in front. **He took me back in time and let me see the moment he had to flee and all that was left behind. He said that camp site still remains to this day and I saw it with my physical eyes as well.**

I saw that on that fateful day (which they knew would happen, for it was prophesied because his people no longer feared God) he had been writing on loose leaf plates (not a stack of them that could, if captured, be confiscated and destroyed). Their camp was centered around a fire, and both he and his companion were smoking pipes. I marveled, for from a modern Mormon viewpoint, smoking could keep a person from going to the temple, which in turn could prevent a person from entering the "Celestial Kingdom." He laughed at such a silly notion, saying it was then part of their culture and everyone did it; it was how the men spent their time.

I also noticed that each person carried with them a small clay pot that doubled as a carrying case for their belongings. When they traveled, their belongings would go in it. It was used for collecting and boiling water, making tea, soup, stew, etc. So, a prized possession everyone had was their pipe and clay pot, and I presume knife and/or jewelry. There is much more that I could share, but I am forbidden from doing so.

Next, he took me north to show me where many Nephite weapon caches remain. There at a bay north of Palmyra he showed me where the Nephites and particularly the Jaredites would travel by ship to get lumber and hunt. This would be the place where the enemy would also come by boat, disembark, and go inland on foot. The banks are naturally occurring higher, but not so high that a person could not walk up them after docking, which, for the Nephites, provided an advantage point to rain down arrows upon the enemy and disable them before they could disembark from their boats.

It was a brilliant strategy, but if they had incorporated fire with it, it would have been even more effective. He said and showed me where many weapons caches were buried and covered in a most brilliant way so as to avoid discovery unless you knew where they were. Indeed, the enemy was so hell-bent on pursuing the Nephites as they fled they never stopped to see what was around them.

He showed me into the future and said that if I disclosed their location to a local archaeologist, he would indeed document their discovery but would wrongly attribute them to the Vikings. It was for this reason that he did not want me to disclose anything at that time, until the narrative of the Book of Mormon is respected and future discoveries on those ancient lands are correctly dated and attributed to the right people.

The last place he wanted me to see was where some of the most horrific torturing of his people took place at that time. This would be one of the most notable evil locations that I was shown; the other was the **Attica Correction Facility** in Attica. The first captured Nephites were kept like trophies by their conquering nation there at the front lines where their troops would land by boat. They were strapped to poles, tortured, but not killed. They were naked, and the incoming troops would take turns mocking, burning, and spitting on them. They were made to endure a long, painful death.

This left such a horrific spiritual scar that modern practitioners of evil use the same area to perform evil acts of the worst kind, including rape, murder, and human sacrifice. That was more than I could take, and I became sick and weakened and could take no more; this is how my trip to western New York came to an end. It is a sad tale of a once powerful and God-fearing nation.

What is Required for More Records?

The brother of Jared asked God to cause six molten stones to emit light so they would have light on their journey to their promised lands. Jesus responded by touching each one, and they did produce light. During this episode, the brother of Jared saw the hand of God and was shocked to learn that man was made in the image of God's spirit body. This initiated a teaching opportunity where Jesus showed him the history of the earth, the future of it, and had him write it down:

> 22 And behold, when ye shall come unto me, **ye shall write them and shall seal them up**, that no one can interpret them; for ye shall write them in a language that they cannot be read.
> 23 And behold, **these two stones will I give unto thee, and ye shall seal them up also with the things which ye shall write.**
> 24 For behold, the language which

ye shall write I have confounded; wherefore I will cause **in my own due time that these stones shall magnify to the eyes of men** these things which ye shall write.

25 And when the Lord had said these words, he **showed unto the brother of Jared all the inhabitants of the earth which had been, and also all that would be;** and he withheld them not from his sight, even unto the ends of the earth.

26 For he had said unto him in times before, that if he would believe in him that he could show unto him all things—it should be shown unto him; therefore the Lord could not withhold anything from him, for he knew that the Lord could show him all things.

27 And the Lord said unto him: **Write these things and seal them up;** and I will show them in mine own due time unto the children of men.

28 **And it came to pass that the Lord commanded him that he**

should seal up the two stones which he had received, and show them not, until the Lord should show them unto the children of men. (Ether 3)

Moroni had the opportunity to read what the brother of Jared saw and was instructed to copy it onto his plates (the gold plates Joseph retrieved) in the brother of Jared's language and Moroni's language. It is commonly referred to as the "sealed portion" of the Book of Mormon.

4 Behold, **I have written upon these plates the very things which the brother of Jared saw;** and **there never were greater things made manifest than those which were made manifest unto the brother of Jared.**
5 Wherefore the **Lord hath commanded me to write them;** and I have written them. And he commanded me that I should seal them up; and he also hath

commanded that I should **seal up the interpretation thereof;** wherefore I have sealed up the interpreters, according to the commandment of the Lord.

Why, according to Moroni, was what was revealed to the brother of Jared "greater than everything else"? Because they contain all the mysteries/revelations of God; the big questions (see numbered points next): Who created God? How was the universe created? What is the real history of the world? etc. Are there any bigger questions than these?

7 And in that day that they shall exercise faith in me, saith the Lord, even as the brother of Jared did, that they may become sanctified **in me,** then will I manifest unto them the things which the brother of Jared saw, even to the unfolding unto them **all my revelations**, saith [1]**Jesus Christ, the** [2]**Son of God, the** [3]**Father of the heavens and of the**

⁴**earth, and ⁵all things that in them are.**

The answer to those mysteries is being held under "lock and key" by God, and only those who first obey the teachings in The Holy Book of Mormon qualify to learn what was revealed to the brother of Jared:

> 8 And he that will **contend against the word of the Lord [Book of Mormon]**, let him be **accursed;** and he that shall deny these things, let him be accursed; for **unto them will I show no greater things,** saith Jesus Christ; for I am he who speaketh. (Ether 4)

Unfortunately, Joseph Smith and Mormon Church leaders have chosen to embrace doctrines that go against The Holy Book of Mormon (e.g., child baptism, polygamy, temple covenants, etc.) and are currently under a curse—**as was foretold:**

54 And your **minds in times past have been darkened because of unbelief,** and because **you have treated lightly the things you have received**—
55 Which vanity and unbelief have **brought the whole church under condemnation.**
56 And this condemnation resteth upon the children of Zion, even all.
57 And **they shall remain under this condemnation until they repent and remember the new covenant, even the Book of Mormon** and the former commandments which I have given them, **not only to say, but to do** according to that which I have written—(D&C 84)

Jesus explained why a person might not embrace His teachings in The Holy Book of Mormon:

11 But **he that believeth these things which I have spoken, him will I visit with the manifestations**

of my Spirit, and he shall know and bear record. For because of my Spirit he shall know that these things are true; for it persuadeth men to do good.

12 And whatsoever thing persuadeth men to do good is of me; for good cometh of none save it be of me. I am the same that leadeth men to all good; **he that will not believe my words [Book of Mormon] will not believe me—** that I am; and he that will not believe me will not believe the Father who sent me. For behold, I am the Father, I am the light, and the life, and the truth of the world. (Ether 4)

Simply put, they do not *truly* believe or have faith in His teachings in The Holy Book of Mormon. For example, does The Holy Book of Mormon contain the full and complete Gospel of Our Lord Jesus Christ? Or does it need new doctrines like those found in the Doctrine & Covenants and the temple? See the difference? True believers in The Holy Book of Mormon have faith that the gospel found in it is sufficient for all their spiritual needs, and God in return bestows His Spirit on them and promises them "greater things":

> 13 Come unto me, O ye Gentiles, and **I will show unto you the greater things,** the **knowledge which is hid up because of unbelief.**
> 14 Come unto me, O ye house of Israel, and it shall be made manifest unto you how **great things the Father hath laid up for you,** from the foundation of the world; and it hath not come unto you, **because of unbelief.** (Ether 4)

Lack of faith in the teachings of The Most Holy Book of Mormon and nothing else is what has prevented Mormons from receiving the promised additional records —be it the sealed portion or any of a number of *other* promised records (e.g., the Plates of Brass, the greater teachings of Jesus, the records of the inhabitants of the Land Northward, etc.). Just to reiterate, additional records have not been given because of disobedience to The Holy Book of Mormon:

> 15 Behold, when ye shall **rend that veil of unbelief [in The Holy Book of Mormon]** which doth cause you to remain in your awful state of wickedness, and hardness of heart, and **blindness of mind [curse of condemnation D&C 84:54]**, then shall the **great and marvelous things** which have been **hid up from the foundation of the world** from you—yea, when ye shall call upon the Father in my name, with a broken heart and a contrite spirit, then shall ye know that the Father hath remembered the covenant which he made unto your fathers, O house of Israel. (Ether 4)

The decreed unfolding of the prophesied records may coincide with the revelations of John, depending on the faithfulness and obedience by believers in

The Holy Book of Mormon:

16 And then shall my revelations which I have caused to be written by my servant **John be UNFOLDED in the EYES of all the people.** Remember, when ye see these things, ye shall know that the time is at hand that **THEY SHALL BE MADE MANIFEST IN VERY DEED.** (Ether 4)

14 And the **heaven DEPARTED as a scroll when it is rolled together;** and every mountain and island were moved out of their places. (Revelation 6)

And:

5 And the **glory of the Lord shall be REVEALED,** and **all flesh shall SEE IT together:** for the mouth of the Lord hath spoken it. (Isaiah 40)

The answer to the question "What is required to bring forth more records?" is faith in The Holy Book of Mormon. How many people will need to reform and become TRUE followers in The Holy Book of Mormon before additional records will be granted is not known (10, 50, the majority?). But the sooner Mormons *do* not just *say* what The Holy Book of Mormon teaches, the sooner they will come out from the curse of condemnation and be able to receive them. To help Mormons obtain this goal, they are encouraged to read *True Points of Doctrine*:

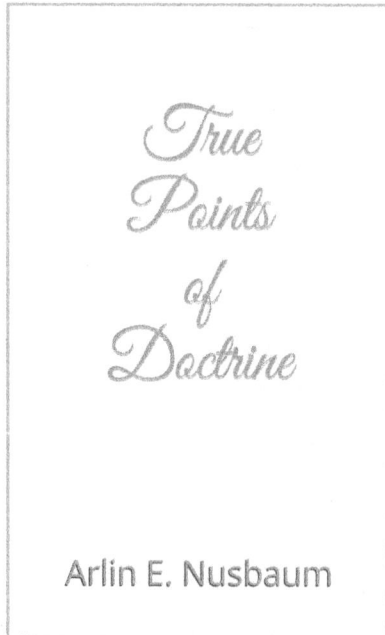

True
Points
of
Doctrine

Arlin E. Nusbaum

I give honor to God for granting me the privilege of serving, working, and learning from His messengers whose purpose is to right wrongs, glorify Our Lord and Savior Jesus Christ, God the Father, and unify His children in preparation for the prophesied *Millennium of Peace*.

Holy, Holy, Holy
Is Our Lord God Almighty
Worthy is the Lamb

Addendum

It's been **4 years** since this book was published (**2016**), and **14 years** since my last experience recounted in *Journey 21* (**2006**) took place. *Journey 20* (2005) and *Journey 21* (2006) allowed me the opportunity to begin documenting the true geography of Book of Mormon lands. I began first on *bomchristian.com* with a more thorough documentation on *bookofmormongeography.org* without ever mentioning those spiritual journeys.

Now, in the year **2020**, I have been blessed with further light and knowledge on certain particulars that were not shown to me during my previous trips and for which I could not ascertain their precise whereabouts.

Having taken myself to much prayer and fasting, I had every confidence that my questions would be answered—if God would allow it, and He did. The glory of God did encompass me, and I was able to see places and events as if I was there. Of course, much has changed the last **1600 years**, and sites have been plowed over and built over many times, but the lay of the land has largely stayed the same.

In particular, I was shown the true location where Our Lord descended in ancient Bountiful as described in 3 Nephi, which is the area surrounding *Delware Park* in *Tonawanda*, and the temple location finely ornamented with the *Albright-Knox Art Gallery*. It was there where Our Lord descended with a host of angels, and it is the place Our Lord will first return at the time of His Second Coming.

> 2 And I John saw the holy city, **new Jerusalem, coming down from God out of heaven**, prepared as a bride adorned for her husband. (Revelation 21)

> 3 And that **IT WAS THE PLACE of the New Jerusalem, which should come down out of heaven**, and the holy sanctuary of the Lord. (Ether 13)

42 He shall manifest himself unto the Gentiles and also unto the Jews, and **the last shall be first**, and the first shall be last. (1 Nephi 13)

Thus, it is important to know where the true geography is in order to know precisely where Our Lord will return *first*. The details of this forthcoming event are in my book *America's Mount Zion* (2020). The *spiritual* interactions will be in ancient Bountiful, and the *political* in Albany, NY.

America's Mount Zion